Larger Than Life

America, a wide-open land with a wide-open heart, needed heroes larger than life. It needed giants like Paul Bunyan, men who embodied the great ideals of a free people.

Hollywood, the dream factory, provided four great giants who believed in and lived truth, justice and the American way. This is their story—and our story as well.

Other Books by
David Hanna

"Come Up and See Me Some Time"
a Confidential Biography of Mae West

"Virginia Hill"
Queen of the Underworld

"Bugsy Siegel"
The Man Who Invented Murder, Inc.

Four Giants Of The West

David Hanna

BELMONT TOWER BOOKS • NEW YORK CITY

For
BACI
With Love

A BELMONT TOWER BOOK

Published by

Tower Publications, Inc.
185 Madison Avenue
New York, N.Y. 10016

PART ONE

Henry Fonda

Years after it was released John Steinbeck told of the lonely night he had looked again at the film of his masterpiece "The Grapes of Wrath" and of the effect he felt, "Time passes and we change; the urgency departs," said Steinbeck, "But I did thread the film on my projector and sat down to weather it out. Then a lean, stringy, dark-faced piece of electric walked out on the screen, and he had me. I believed my own story again. It was fresh and happening and good."

*H*enry Fonda, an American theatrical giant, was at the turning point of his career in the spring of 1934 when he walked briskly along Fifth Avenue to an appointment at the Gotham Hotel with Marc Connelly, one of the era's most distinguished playwrights and directors. Connelly was a round, friendly, talkative man who had won a Pulitzer Prize and earned a bundle with *The Green Pastures* a few years earlier. Success had not affected the warmth of his personality or his gentle humanity and love for people. Connelly was a rare gentleman in the hurly burly world of the Broadway theatre. For all his grace and charm, he was a shrewd theatrical craftsman with a keen eye for talent even if his way of displaying it was somewhat unorthodox.

Young Fonda found this out when he was greeted in Connelly's suite and given a comfortable arm chair while Connelly pulled out the script of his newest play, *The Farmer Takes a Wife,* which was to have a summer stock tryout with the Westchester Players at Mount Kisco, New York, during the summer.

Fonda wasn't exactly a household word to New York or to Connelly, but he wasn't a stranger either. There were more Fonda enthusiasts around the Great White Way than the young actor suspected. What little had been seen of him had placed him in that special category of "young actors to watch." Performers, even before their own talent has been acclaimed, have a way of recognizing stars.

Connelly suggested that he was going to read the first few pages in order to give Fonda an idea of the play, but to the younger man's surprise, the white-haired playwright read on and on—having the time of his life, playing out all the parts, embellishing them with accents and gestures.

Connelly, like many writers working in the theatre, Sinclair Lewis, Thornton Wilder, Alexander Woollcott and George S. Kaufman, would have preferred being an actor to a writer. Fonda, grasping the situation, reacted whenever Connelly paused at a dramatic point or a joke. Fonda applauded or laughed accordingly.

It took Connelly two hours to finish the reading. Glancing at his watch he explained that he had an appointment, wouldn't have time to listen to Fonda read. "You see Max Gordon (top Broadway producer) tomorrow and he'll sign you," said Connelly. "How much do you want?" Fonda, whose salary had ranged from twenty-five to thirty-five dollars a week, said he didn't know what to ask. Connelly leaned over to him confidentially and said, "Ask him for two hundred a week and don't take a cent less."

The summer of 1934 was an extraordinary year in summer stock, a comparatively new theatrical innovation. The economic conditions of the Great Depression had lured the biggest Broadway names to the hinterlands and the resort areas where barns had been converted into playhouses. Most were playing week-long engagements of their old hits at salaries little more than Fonda was advised to ask of Max Gordon. Lenore Ulric was heating up the barns in *Pagan Lady,* Tom Powers starred in the thriller, *Ten Minute Alibi,* Francine Larrimore tried out *Spring Song* and other stars on the circuit were Ernest Truex, Spring Byington, Gertrude Lawrence and Irene Purcell. Even the legendary Laurette Taylor had been lured out of her self-imposed retirement.

Tryouts were more keenly watched by Broadwayites than revivals and word quickly spread around the summer circuit that there was a lean, lanky young fellow knocking them dead at Mount Kisco in *The Farmer Takes a Wife* opposite the well-liked star June Walker.

The play was pleasant, but that was the best that could be said for it, being very much in the Connelly genre, quiet, well-written, wry, humorous, actionless. It emerged as a slow motion picture of life along the Erie Canal at the turn of the century. The plot involved the efforts of a farmer to lure a canal cook away from waterfront life to marriage and the quiet of his farm. The cook, played by June Walker, was like a young Tugboat Annie, a rough and ready charmer.

It was one of those "b'gosh" things, unpretentious, needing all the atmosphere Max Gordon's handsome production provided and every ounce of talent its performers could provide. Gordon, like Sam Goldwyn, was a man who took pride in his craft; so the cast was excellent, including two great names of vaudeville's past, Herb Williams and Kate Mayhew.

All the players were duly noted by the critics and June Walker, who had never gotten a poor review in her life, received the praise everyone expected. But when it came to audience reaction to Connelly's slice of Americana, attention was riveted on the tall kid from Grand Island, Nebraska, whose long, dark lashes highlighted dazzling blue eyes. Fonda was twenty-four, and oozed sex appeal as he loped awkwardly through the performance creating such a natural characterization that if he sneezed by accident it would integrate into the character.

But the matinee crowd didn't give a damn about Fonda's art. They were telling one another, "Forget the play. Just look at the new boy. He's dazzling." As much as any other element, the chatter about the newcomer helped *Farmer* hobble along to a respectable run of one hundred and five performances.

Its fragile success and Fonda's triumph were greeted with whoops of joy wherever young actors gathered in the thirties, the Astor Hotel lobby, Walgreen's drug store at 45th and Broadway, agents' offices, LeBlanc's cut-rate ticket agency and at the Rehearsal Club (for girls), a couple of whose guests had dated Fonda.

In the eight years Fonda had been in the theatre, working as an odd-job amateur and eventually, a professional in stock, he'd accumulated a host of friends—and admirers—whose names today read like a section of *Who's Who*. But in the thirties the majority were, like Fonda, struggling young actors, swapping quarters and hustling "catsup sandwiches" at the automat—two slices of buttered bread for a nickel at the machines, catsup on the house at the tables. His close pals included Jimmy Stewart, director Joshua Logan, Imogene Coca, Kent Smith, Humphrey Bogart, director Bretaigne Windust, Dorothy McGuire, and the better known Margaret Sullavan.

Fonda married Sullavan in 1931, but the marriage was short-lived. Although it lasted less than a year, Maggie and Hank remained friends until the end of her life, which seemed to have been filled with more tragedy than it deserved. Strangely, so has Henry Fonda's. His private life has never possessed that aura of purpose, success and clarity that has made the actor's career so distinctive. His career shows growth at every stage and Fonda's art has steadily matured from great young parts like Tom Joad in John Steinbeck's *Grapes of*

Wrath, to Clarence Darrow, the criminal lawyer who thundered his way into legal history.

At the time Fonda was stirring up things at the Garrick theatre, I was working at the Sardi building hustling copy for a publicity office, carrying the title of "planter"—a refined occupational description of "messenger." Like those who knew him, after seeing *Farmer* I wished the young actor's first hit had been in something stronger. Fonda had his own ideas about things, "I'm suspicious of anything that happens too fast or too soon."

I worked with Henry Fonda many years later but never got close to him. There was no reason to. We maintained a cordial and workmanlike relationship while I was the publicity man on the Rome-based production of *War and Peace*, the King Vidor version in which Audrey Hepburn played Natasha and Fonda was Pierre. When I met him I felt that I had already known and admired him for many years. Watching his professionalism at first hand enhanced the respect I already felt.

I had seen virtually every one of his plays and never ceased to marvel at his technique, the magic of his understated style. His style of action was called "effortless" and "casual" but he had worked a lifetime to achieve it. Fonda believes in creating a real character, not a performer; "I don't want the wheels to show." Of course I was familiar with the best of his movies as well as the bombs that were every actor's lot in those days.

Actors at that time signed seven year contracts

and often had to take parts that didn't suit them. Fonda, a real professional, did his best with every role, but some of them just didn't fit.

So when a writer sits down to do a piece on Fonda he totes out all the superlatives he has been warned to avoid during his apprenticeship in newspapering—finest, greatest, etc. Happily, they all apply to the art of Henry Fonda.

Statistically his record of achievements is impressive—79 starring roles in films, 16 appearances on Broadway, numerous TV shows and a belated London debut as *Darrow* that drew a standing ovation night after night for an actor, at the peak of his talents, aged seventy, and wearing a pacemaker in a heart that had finally wound down a trifle.

There can be little argument in calling Henry Fonda one of the finest actors America has ever produced or in agreeing with *Current Biography* which notes in its opening paragraph: "If any actor can be said nearly to embody the ideal American, it is Henry Fonda, the veteran of eighty motion pictures and of the theatre and television. During a career spanning half a century he has come to embody, in the words of Joshua Logan, 'a kind of synthesis of all the heroes of Mark Twain, Bret Harte, James Fenimore Cooper, Hawthorne, Poe and Irving'."

For an idea of the sex exuded by young Fonda back in the thirties and forties, there's the following from *Modern Screen:* "Hank, with his black hair and his blazing blue eyes was easily one of the best looking members of the company

(University Players at Cape Cod). He seemed almost ashamed of his good looks. He always wore the oldest and most disreputable clothes an old suit, a sleeveless sweater and trousers cut off at the knee.

"Though Hank's a husky young man, to look at him, you'd never guess that in strength he's a regular Hercules. Once when a sedan went over on its side, Henry got out of the car, braced his back and without any help from the other passengers, pushed the sedan out of the sand and onto the road."

Maybe it was best summed up at a radio broadcast I attended, one of those Louella Parsons affairs where stars did scenes from their new pictures. Hank was sitting at the edge of the stage, his long legs hanging over the apron, reading the script. The pretty young thing next to me sighed, "You know, if Marlene Dietrich ever saw those eyelashes she'd either kill him or rape him."

* * *

From Grand Island to Nebraska where Henry Fonda was born, May 16, 1905, to Broadway and Hollywood, there lay a straight road, with only a few pot holes, now and then, consisting largely of latching on to enough money to pay room rent and eat. In the depression days of Fonda's early career he was sailing in a big boat; being broke, poor or unemployed was no disgrace. Struggling young actors and men two decades older who had been toppled from executive jobs were all in trouble.

In an autobiographical article for the *New Yorker* later reprinted in the *Reader's Digest,* Fonda wrote: "Acting is putting on a mask. The worst torture that can happen to me is not having a mask to get in back of..

'I am the oldest of three. My sisters, Harriet and Jayne, are married to businessmen. My father, William Brace Fonda, owned a printing company in Omaha where I was raised. He died in 1935. My mother, an angelic woman, died the year before. I look like my father. There is a strong Fonda look..It's in my sisters, in their children, and in my children. My son, Peter grew in the same way. He stands six feet two—an inch taller than I am.

Fonda's childhood clearly was a happy one, typical of its time, free of the nerves and tensions that touch young people today. Living in Omaha, surrounded by a family, strong in the unifying traditions of their Italian-Dutch heritage, Fonda looks back upon his youth with affectionate memories.

"We swam naked in sand pits and built shacks out of lumber we stole off construction jobs. As a kid, I'd go downtown on the streetcar to my father's office, and he'd give me a nickel to go to the nickelodeon, where I saw the early Charlie Chaplin and William S. Hart pictures. Starting when I was twelve, I worked in my father's printshop in the summers, at two dollars a week. When I was going to high school, I always worked in the summers. It never occurred to me to question it; I just assumed I'd have to work. My mother was a Christian Scientist. My grandmother was a

Second Reader in the church. Dorothy Brando, Marlon's mother, an amateur actress, was a close friend of Mother's in and out of the church

"I started out wanting to be a writer. At ten, I wrote a story called "The Mouse," which was told from a mouse's point of view. We were living in a suburb of Omaha called Dundee and the story was published in the Dundee newspaper. I took up journalism at college, at the University of Minnesota, and I worked at two jobs while studying— trouble-shooter for the Northwestern Bell Telephone Company, and director of various sports and other activities at a settlement house in town. I'd take the streetcar from the campus to the settlement house, on the other side of town, in temperatures that went as low as thirty below zero, and in the summer I played baseball and taught tennis. I got thirty dollars a month, plus room and board. Dad sent me ten bucks a week. It was exhausting. I did it for a year, and then I went home for a rest. While I was home, I got a message from Do Brando to call Gregory Foley, the director of the Omaha Community Playhouse. She knew that I was at loose ends, and that I was the right age and type to play a juvenile lead they were looking for. I called Foley, and was told to come over to his headquarters—a studio with a skylight, which was kind of bohemian for Omaha. Foley, a short, red-headed Irishman, handed me the published version of *You and I,* by Philip Barry, and asked me to read the part of Ricky, the juvenile lead. First thing I knew, I was cast in the play. I was sure I didn't want to do it. At rehearsals, I

Henry Fonda, everyone knew, was headed for stardom, even when he was a "nobody" on Broadway.

found myself in another world. I was the kind of guy who thinks everybody is looking at *him*. I was very reluctant. I had no ambition to be an actor. But it was summer, and I had nothing else to do, so I joined the company. I stayed as an actor with the Playhouse for two nine-month seasons and did four principal roles. I practically lived at the theatre. I painted scenery, soaked up the sight of the lines of rope that go up to the grid, smelled greasepaint, smelled smells I had never smelled before. My parents weren't particularly for it, but they accepted it."

Young Fonda, who had long been nicknamed "Hank" got a job with a retail credit company in 1926 and was doing fine—just learning the ropes and showing promise of a bright future when he heard from Foley again. "He wanted to know if I would play the lead in *Merton of the Movies,* a stock standard farce by George S. Kaufman and Marc Connelly that had made a star out of Glenn Hunter. Fonda, Sr. vetoed the idea but Hank was twenty-one and had his own mind. This led to a rift between father and son which lasted until the reviews came out and an Omaha paper ran a banner: "Who Needs Glenn Hunter? We have Henry."

The dizzy success of his one week engagement as Merton decided Hank about his career and the next years were spent in apprentice jobs with various companies in New England, playing bits, painting scenery, distributing window cards but getting to know people as well. Stars like Laura Hope Crews, Peggy Wood and Romney Brent—as well as kids like Jimmy Stewart and Maggie Sullavan.

Eventually Hank felt he was good enough to tackle New York. "I was damn sure I was a good actor and sure eventually that I was going to prove it. I learned I was good when I played *Merton* in Omaha. Even today I can remember how I felt. There was a kind of breathless feeling I couldn't ever recapture. It was like being ten years old and playing cops and robbers."

He found a ten-dollar-a-week room on 114th Street, joined Actors Equity, and made the rounds of agents. "I became the best unknown actor in town. I didn't present myself well to producers." This was understandable. Producers weren't used to kids with a Nebraska twang, who slouched their six-feet-two frames or who preferred the casual look to slicked-down hair, button-down collars, the Windsor knot, and cuff links favored by most theatrical aspirants of the day. And frankly there weren't many plays around looking for Fonda types. Until he established a track record, Fonda got what he expected—the brushoff, waiting patiently for the long arm of coincidence.

Then, in the spring of 1934, he had his first big break when he did a sketch with Imogene Coca in a Broadway revue, *New Faces of 1934*. Some critics noticed him and called the two a promising comedy team, and as a result of the show Leland Hayward became his agent and manager. Hayward thought Fonda was a natural for the movies, and kept asking him to go to Hollywood to meet producer Walter Wanger. But Fonda, who felt that he was just starting to do well in the theater, wasn't interested. Nevertheless Hayward was persistent, and since Wanger was paying expenses, the actor flew out to Hollywood.

Fonda decided to make his price so high that Wanger wouldn't take him; since he was making $100 a week in New York, he would ask for an exorbitant $350 a week. During a lengthy conference, he kept insisting on staying with the theater, so Wanger guaranteed that he could spend a few months every year on Broadway. Fonda was still about to spring his $350 idea when he heard Wanger offering $1,000 a week. He later said that he was so dazed that he didn't remember having signed the contract.

For an actor who had it made at the very beginning, Hank retained reservations about Hollywood and the movies, and they have stayed with him from the day he started until the present. Of his first picture, *The Farmer Takes a Wife,* playing opposite Janet Gaynor, Hank said, "It was easy to make the transition to movies. I started to act as I had in the play and Victor Fleming, the director, told me I was mugging, that's all it took. I just pulled it down to reality. You don't project anything for movies. You do it as you would in your own back yard. Because of all the experience back of me in the part it didn't bother me to work out of continuity, the way you do in making a movie. Of course, there's very little personal satisfaction in doing those bits and pieces. You don't really have any recollection of having created a role. But the money was attractive."

So were the circumstances under which Fonda landed in Hollywood. There were no years of struggling or bit parts, no buildup to stardom. Fonda was almost a star in his first film. Although in all but one of the eighteen films he made before *Young Mr. Lincoln* he was billed beneath at least one other performer, and although he was usually the foil for someone in a more spectacular part, he never had anything but a major role.

But the price of stardom came high. "One movie I was eager to do was *Grapes of Wrath*—the part of Tom Joad—and I had to sign a seven-year contract with Twentieth Century Fox to get it. I made all kinds of movies I hated. My gorge rises when I remember them."

That statement was made several years ago. Hank Fonda wasn't the first actor to complain about Hollywood and he was far from the last. For all I know he may still be beefing about the tough lot of a movie star in the days of Louis B. Mayer, Jack Warner and Darryl Zanuck, who forced Fonda into a long-term deal as the price of Tom Joad. But when a newspaper interviewer recently asked Fonda why he could be found all over the TV screen doing commericals with all the vigor of his best screen or stage performance, Fonda's answer was the realistic one to be expected of an artist who has tried—successfully—to play square with himself and his public.

"Two things led me to commercials. Money, of course. They pay well: there are the residuals and if I didn't do things like that I wouldn't be able to live as I have—raising a family, putting the children through college, travelling as I like, living in New

York and having a house on the Riviera. And doing a play whenever I can. An actor has to face his practical problems just like anyone else. Money is a practical problem. So is exposure. The actor without exposure isn't there, he's not around; you don't hear about him. And that's not healthy for his career, his ego or his growth."

So perhaps, in retrospect, the bomb movies of his long career no longer hurt, and he can look back on the great ones with satisfaction.

But Fonda was obliged to wait for them to come along—and eventually to battle for them. All things considered, Hank was an awfully patient guy.

In the light of the era of Fonda's early career, the enthusiasm of his agent, Leland Hayward, in landing him with Walter Wanger seemed perfectly logical. Hayward represented a new breed of theatrical agent, educated, witty, suave, smooth, with taste and good manners. In a phrase, he didn't smoke cigars. Wanger, too, was something new in the Hollywood scene, a young man, college-educated who had made such an impression running production for Paramount in the East that they brought him to Hollywood and created a unit especially for him.

Fonda was one of the first actors he signed, and Wanger began earning a return on his investment by lending him out, first for *Farmer;* then to Twentieth again for *Way Down East,* which was pretty awful as a silent movie even though it enjoyed the direction of D.W. Griffith and the acting of Lillian Gish. Fonda's leading lady was Rochelle Hudson who replaced Janet Gaynor, taken ill, either legitimately or from having read the script. Hank was again a farmer—this time the son of a hypocrite of a father who, learning of Rochelle's scarlet past, turns her off his property in the middle of a blizzard. Hank dashes to her rescue, grabbing her unconscious body from an ice block in the river seconds before it breaks.

More than talent was involved in Fonda's surviving *Way Down East*. His looks, for one thing; Hank's boyish handsomeness led fans to want to know about and see more of that "country boy." Homespun characters had come to be played exclusively for laughs on the screen, perhaps because there hadn't been a star around to play them since Richard Barthelemess grew older and Richard Cromwell drifted away from the Hollywood scene. Fonda, clearly was a young actor with range and fans, as they always do, sensed that he would be around for a long, long time.

But no thanks to Walter Wanger who, after all the *wunderkind* hoopla died down, turned out to be one of Hollywood's most erratic producers, a man who talked art, message pictures and social significance out of one side of his mouth and made junk with the other—films like *Salome, Where She Dances* starring Yvonne de Carlo which was probably vastly more entertaining than his gigantic finale flop, *Cleopatra*. It may or may not be significant that while Walter Wanger was attending college, Darryl Zanuck was writing *Rin Tin Tin* scripts on the kitchen table of his Hollywood pull-down bed apartment—and those stories still hold up in silent movie festivals.

There are some great credits in Wanger's list—

and they all happened when strong-minded directors came along and "barred him from the set." One such tyrant was Fritz Lang who took Fonda out of the hayloft in *You Only Live Once* and out onto the streets where, with the feel of cement under his feet, Fonda turned in a masterful performance as an ex-convict, determined to go straight against the tragic odds of his past, a trapped creature in Lang's nightmare world of cold, implacable fate.

Interviewers who talked to Fonda in recent years have expressed surprise that the star, an admitted perfectionist, has not overcome his dislike of Lang, saying that he hated Lang and recalling that the martinet pinched actors to obtain reactions. "He was too preoccupied with what everything was going to look like." Lang, of course, is very much a cult these days; as a matter of fact, he always was, but the legacy of extraordinary movies he left behind doesn't justify an unpleasant personality. Few actors ever got along with Lang and there were top stars who flatly refused to work with him.

Still, he did more for Fonda's career than the producer who signed his pay check. Wanger loaned him around town as though Fonda were a second rate stock player, and the record is shocking proof of the man's ineptness—things like *Slim*, in which Hank got into overalls and became a farm boy again, *That Certain Woman*, a remake of a tear-jerker that had marked Gloria Swanson's debut as a talking actress, a story unimproved by years. He appeared opposite Bette Davis in

Jezebel, Bette Davis' answer to David O. Selznick for rejecting her for Scarlett O'Hara in *Gone with the Wind,* ostensibly because he wanted Errol Flynn as Rhett Butler and Bette wouldn't stand still for that. She liked Flynn personally; he amused her vastly, but she considered the playboy Aussie not in her league professionally—not up to Rhett Butler, for sure.

Only Bette and Jack Warner know the truth of the story—and Bette sticks to it. The other major Scarlett contenders have gone to that great Tara in the sky, Tallulah, Susan Hayward, as well as Scarlett herself, Vivien Leigh. Time seems to give more and more credence to the story that Vivien had long been chosen for Scarlett and the casting marathon only lent zest to the game—as did *Jezebel.*

Selznick, whose office was always thickly carpeted because in fits of temper he used to fall on the floor, beat his head and kick his feet, fussed and fumed that Warners was behaving unprofessionally in making *Jezebel,* which he labelled a "quickie imitation of GWTW." *Jezebel* won Bette an Oscar, made a fortune, and Hank enjoyed the best exposure of his career. Fonda was at his best in a thankless role, Bette's stiff-necked suitor, a New Orleans banker, who reluctantly bows out of her life, returning, after a decent interval, with a wife. Bette's lust for revenge stirs up a mountain of bubbles as the soap opera churns along to a climax which gives Bette the opportunity to repent her perverse past.

Hank's bachelor status did a lot for his standing

with the fans, as it did for his old pal, Jimmy Stewart. Jimmy's rise in Hollywood coincided with Hank's, and both young men found themselves linked in the columns with gals they'd never met. They shrugged off the misrepresentation of their amorous capacities and appeared to enjoy grabbing the money while they could, even if Hank was moodier about his sloppy parts than Jimmy.

Both men enjoyed tying one on now and then, but the pacing of movie making in those days was against protracted benders. Fonda, for example, starred in thirty-four pictures in the eight years between his debut and 1942 when he enlisted as an apprentice seaman in the Navy at the age of thirty-seven. In his own story, Hank sums up his Navy experience briefly. "I served as quartermaster third class on a destroyer in the Pacific. Later, the Executive Officer of the destroyer recommended me for a commission; I was discharged and then immediately commissioned as a Lieutenent J.G." He served as an assistant operations and air combat intelligence officer under Admiral John Hoover, earning a Bronze Star and a Presidential citation. In October, 1945, Hank was discharged as a lieutenant, senior grade.

* * *

He was already wondering if he would ever return to movies and Hollywood; his heart and his interests lay with the theatre. But whatever his postwar decision, there was plenty of public interest in bachelor Fonda in the arena where it

Fonda found a gravy train in Westerns, scoring in "Jesse James" and "My Darling Clementine."

counted, among the fans. The movie magazines had found it impossible to ignore Hank, even if the writers, who always enjoyed his cooperation, found him a tough guy to write about. He simply didn't lead the bachelor life the town expected. An actor who dashed from picture to picture really hadn't much time for the night club route. Fonda didn't go to the races. He did few of the things that made good pictures and interesting fan magazine stories. But the fan mags substituted speculation—even if he was seldom seen with any of the "in" glamor girls.

Hank, though, became a popular subject for "beefcake" art. He was a good swimmer, with a swimmer's physique, lean, sinewy, not muscle-bound. So there were plenty of photos around showing Hank "at home and at play."

They had a field day, albeit a brief one, when Wanger, using Hank in one of his own pictures for a change, teamed him with ex-wife Margaret Sullavan in *The Moon's Our Home,* a screwball comedy no better or worse than anything to bear the Wanger imprint. The gossips pondered the probability that the picture would bring about a reconcilation with Maggie. Not quite. Both were involved in plans for second marriages.

Maggie married Hank's agent, Leland Hayward. In 1936 Fonda announced his marriage to Frances Seymour Brokaw, a socialite, twenty-eight-year-old widow he had met in England, mother of a five-year-old daughter. There were congratulations all around, even if his close friends wondered how the homespun Fonda would ever make it as the husband of a worldly, sophisticated woman. She simply didn't fit into Fonda's way of life, but they seemed happy enough and pals felt that, at thirty-one, Fonda, weary of bachelorhood, decided marriage was a convention he needed at this stage of his life.

Their first child, Jane Seymour, was born on December 21, 1937, during the filming of *Jezebel,* and Peter was born three years later, in 1940, concurrent with the release of *Grapes of Wrath.*

From the beginning the marriage of Frances Brokaw and Henry Fonda had an aura of secrecy surrounding it, and the public really only became aware that it existed when the children were born and in 1939 when Jane was believed to be the victim of a kidnap plot—a scheme overheard by a young woman in San Bernadino who relayed it to the police. They took it seriously enough to post a twenty-four hour guard around the Fonda's Beverly Hills home. The plot, if it failed with Jane, had an alternative—kidnapping the star himself. That it wasn't a hoax was substantiated by the fact that the threatening kidnappers, aware the girl had overheard their conversation, warned her "to keep her mouth shut or look forward to a new face."

Almost from the beginning of the marriage there were rumors of rifts and separation, set at rest as each child was born. There were hints that the socialite wife, suffering from acute depression, spent considerable time in institutions. Josh Logan once said, "Frances was not really interested in the theatre, so she was always embarrassed to talk about it. She'd talk of operations, jewelry, the stock market. I often wondered what she and Henry talked about, because these are the only subjects Henry couldn't talk about."

Henry, very much a private man at the time and for a long while afterward, shared his dismay at the turn the marriage had taken with no one. It remained for his children, Peter and Jane, to draw him out of his shell years later when, as rebellious young adults, they shocked him, literally cornering him into playing a role he'd ignored too long—a human being.

"Hank was always a fascinating guy, someone so frank and honest that he sometimes seemed rude, but, then, there was all that reserve no one could explain. He was outgoing and gregarious but only in those areas that interested him. He refused to step outside his narrow world. Today it's a whole new ball game. Fonda's fun, real fun. It may sound far out, but I think he's living his youth all over again through his kids and wishing he'd enjoyed their freedom and knew as much as they do."

But the Flying Fondas were still tiny tots before the war while Hank combined the grubby business of making the right kind of contract with his desire to settle into the kind of movie making his talents entitled him to.

Fortunately for Fonda, Paramount had had it with Walter Wanger and he transferred his production unit to United Artists, a company so short of product it would have welcomed anything. Wanger chose to concentrate on making a star out of Hedy Lamarr and then, because she was under contract to Metro and unavailable to him, he had his wife, Joan Bennett, dye her hair black to play Lamarr-type roles. Now and then John Ford dropped by the Wanger plant, kept the producer locked up in his office, and did a *Stage Coach* or a *Long Voyage Home.* Alfred Hitchcock gave Wanger *Foreign Correspondent.* Hank kept busy "on the road" hustling from studio to studio on loan-out. He worked at 20th Century-Fox so frequently that it was assumed he belonged there.

Henry King, the director who, like Fonda, had taken a beating for *Way Down East,* found a way to make things up to Hank by costarring him with Tyrone Power in *Jesse James.* They formed a fascinating team, and King knew his way through action scenes and outdoor drama. The film was a hit, and Fonda fans saw him in a new light, grown out of overalls and light comedies into a strong, taciturn two-gun outdoor character. The role, less colorful than Power's flamboyant Jesse James, came across as the more interesting because of Fonda's capacity for making any part he played, even the slop, a three-dimensional character. You not only saw Frank James pursuing his trade. You knew what made him tick.

Inevitably, Fonda and director John Ford would come together, and *Young Mr. Lincoln* spawned their association. Hank wasn't willing to tackle the big Lincoln, the presidential years, but he could see himself as the young man, between the ages of twenty-three and thirty; his first encounter with politics and his tragic romance with Ann Rutledge, the practice of law, and the flowering of his romance with Mary Todd.

Young Mr. Lincoln was a beautiful picture, a

masterpiece for Ford and Fonda as well as the rest of the cast. And Twentieth Century-Fox gave it one of the few Hollywood premieres notable for its grace and dignity. Marion Anderson, at the height of her vocal powers and fame, sang a brief concert before the picture unreeled and as they left the black tie audience realized they had finally seen a major star fulfill his promise.

Grapes of Wrath, John Steinbeck's chilling saga of the migratory workers of the thirties, became the next Ford-Fonda collaboration. Fonda was Steinbeck's choice as well as Ford's, but Tyrone Power, the studio's top male star, wanted the meaty role of Tom Joad. This was the part which forced Hank into a seven year contract with 20th-Century. At the time it seemed worth it. Wrote critic Peter Cowie; "It is Fonda, with his cat-like walk and his deep etched eyes gaze, who takes on the features of an Everyman, suffering with grace and every so often lashing out against exploitation."

Years later John Steinbeck said of Fonda: "Time passes and we change; the urgency departs. But I threaded the film on my projector and sat back to weather it out. Then a lean, stringy, dark-faced piece of electric walked out on the screen, and he had me. I believed my own story again. It was fresh and happening and good."

Grapes of Wrath was not a boxoffice success; nor was it expected to be. It was one of those pictures Hollywood's big studios turned out now and then, much as TV networks give over Sunday to discussion and educational programs—films designed to display their social consciousness and realization that there was another world outside the tinsel and plaster-of-paris studios nestled in the hills of Southern California.

They spent as little as possible on these adventures and after you got beyond Fonda and Ford you realized how deliberately they'd played it safe—recruiting a totally inept supporting cast of stock players like Jane Darwell and Charley Grapewin to play the senior Joads and filling the rest of the parts with stock players. Even John Carradine, under a Fox contract, always a fine actor, seemed uncomfortable. Any road company troupe of *Tobacco Road* players could have done better and when Fox, years later, made *Tobacco Road* and threw the part of Jeeter Lester to Grapewin, an extremely old man, I wondered why no one ever had thought of Hank Fonda. The actors who first played Jeeter, Henry Hull and James Barton, were then in their forties and no one at Fox seemed to realize that in those Southern hills, kids marry young and a fella can be a grandpappy at thirty-five.

Fonda had another crack at a good Western part before he entered the Navy—in *The Return of Frank James* which was all his although it involved working with Fritz Lang again. Fonda was no happier this time around than before, summing up his experience tersely, "He killed horses." Another major Fonda piece was *The Ox-Bow Incident,* foisted on the studio by William Wellman who sold them a bill of goods while lynching was in the news. It was stark, realistic drama, the first message western; Fonda was superb and, of course, today it ranks as a classic.

When Hank turned in the key to his dressing room to join the Navy, there were many fine accomplishments for him to ruminate about during his tenure at Fox but, being an actor and a human, he couldn't quite overlook, forgive or forget *Alexander Graham Bell* in which he stooged for Don Ameche, *Lillian Russell,* a musical into which he fitted like a wrong note. And there were quite a few others. He had to realize that he was obliged to return to the contract after his period of service although the studio would lose its claim on the time he spent in the Navy. There were also those years with Walter Wanger to recall with horror. He'd returned to Broadway only once in his Hollywood career—and that had been a disappointment. If there was resolve in his attitude as he got into uniform, Hank was damned sure that wasn't going to happen the second time around—assuming there was a second time around for him in the movies.

As the big stars like Gable, Stewart, Fonda, Tyrone Power, Melvyn Douglas, Robert Montgomery and others vacated dressing rooms for barracks none of them could count on the future. They'd been around long enough to be aware of the fickle attitude of the public and the indifference of studios to anyone who started looking like a loser. In the silent days and right through the thirties, a star's life, like a dog's, was figured to last about seven years. Dogs had begun to live longer because of better food, conscientious care and vitamins.

About all the stars could depend on were vitamins and food.

* * *

For most Americans involved in World War II, their careers were prologues to the war itself. For Henry Fonda the war was the prologue to his work. He climbed out of his Navy blues, perhaps sighing a bit at the prospect of returning to fill the remaining years of his contract. *My Darling Clementine*, which reunited him with John Ford, was the only conspicuous success to come out of his immediate postwar assignments. It was a solid Western, filled with Ford's characteristic touches, strong action, and man-to-man conflicts. The film served to reinforce Fonda's standing at the box office. He was still a big name—especially in the western field where it counted, and that, from a financial viewpoint, meant more than losing an Academy Award nomination for Tom in *Grapes of Wrath* to old pal James Stewart, who nabbled it for an inferior performance in *The Philadelphia Story*. Jane Darwell and John Ford both were honored for the Steinbeck saga of the dust bowl and Stewart was the first to claim that "Hank wuz robbed." He had voted for his friend himself.

Hank wasn't exactly a clock-watcher, but beginning in 1947, as his contract neared its end, the actor knew the pay-off was at hand. He'd found the piece he had been waiting for all these years— the vehicle that would take him back to the theatre, not as a visiting movie star, but as the Broadway

35

actor he had planned to be in his youth. Never one to turn up his nose at auditorium appearances nor to downgrade little theatre or Off Broadway, Fonda was mature and traditional enough to work for a piece of the action in a hit play along the theatrical world's most discriminating avenue, Broadway.

One of Hank's old friends from the stock company days was Joshua Logan, who had carved a successful career as a director, mainly in the theatre. He co-directed one of Fonda's films, *I Met My Love Again,* with Arthur Ripley, a fabled behind-the-camera man whose career dated back to the Keystone Kops. Josh put together *Where's Charley,* the musical version of *Charlie's Aunt* starring Ray Bolger in exactly four weeks. On the fourth week of rehearsal the performance was locked up and never altered afterward. It was a fantastic accomplishment, probably without precedent.

When Fonda visited New York in 1947, Josh showed him an adaptation of Thomas Heggen's best seller, *Mr. Roberts,* Leland Hayward intended being the play's producer and without admitting it to one another all the play's creators, Heggens, Joshua Logan and Hayward had Fonda in mind from the beginning.

Roberts is the first officer of a cargo ship, the Reluctant, a thousand miles from the war. He wants to get off the ship and into combat before it is too late. But his tyrannical captain refuses his request for a transfer. An affectionate crew does the job for him and the denouement, inevitably, is

William Powell, Henry Fonda and Jack Lemmon in film of Fonda's stage hit, Mr. Roberts.

the message that Mr. Roberts has been killed in action.

"It was like being in love," recalls Fonda. "You had good feelings as soon as you read the script, and they never went away." Fonda didn't dawdle over accepting the part and went into rehearsal with a superb cast, especially Robert Keith. Fonda's scenes with Keith wrote an acting page seldom equalled in Broadway annals.

The opening night audience on February 18, 1948, expected something magnificent and they weren't disappointed. It was as though Henry Fonda had never gone away, as though he'd been on Broadway all those years, right where he belonged. Thunderous applause greeted the first sight of him, and there was an ovation at the finish. No doubt about it, *Mr. Roberts* was an artistic and commercial success, and Fonda had established his right to be called one of our "first actors." He needed *Mr. Roberts* for just this purpose, to stake his claim—an American play with the aura of a classic. Fonda could never have succeded in the classics—not with his thin, nasal voice, his mid-Western twang, so he wisely never considered them. *Mr. Roberts* became his own "classic"—the first. Two more "Fondas" were still to come.

Hank was forty-three and enjoying every bit of the sweet smell of success, success that belonged to him night after night and twice a day on matinee days. He never let up on a performance, nor did any of his fellow actors. They blended into an ensemble troupe making it impossible for one to ever let up.

Henry and Frances took a house in Connecticut. They were glad to be back in the East where the world they knew was natural—not the imitation Pennsylvania-style farmhouse they had built during the years in Brentwood.

The children were discovering their father and Jane had no idea of his profession until she asked her mother why he sometimes wore a beard and discovered that he was an actor. Hank became a cautious Sunday artist, even sculpting Peter's head.

Plans to film the play with the original cast in 1949 fell through. Undeterred, Fonda continued right on playing. The house was sold out night after night and professionally the triumph was everything he'd dreamed of. At home, the serenity he felt at the theatre was missing. Tensions between Hank and Frances became more apparant and this was the point when her long periods at rest homes could no longer be kept secret. Her condition was widely known in theatrical circles and people began to understand the Fonda mystique a little better. They understood the reserve that had intensified throughout the years of the marriage.

Divorce proceedings were announced in 1949; shortly afterward, Frances went to an institution. On August 11, 1950, no one, including Henry, was prepared for the lurid headlines: FONDA'S WIFE, ILL, COMMITS SUICIDE AT REST HOME—SLASHES HER THROAT.

Joshua Logan said that Fonda played *Mr. Roberts* that night "to keep from going crazy." For Fonda, the hurt grew more public when Frances' will included the children and pointedly left out Henry. As far as Jane and Peter were concerned, they were told their mother had died of a heart attack in the hospital. Jane learned the truth a year later from reading a fan magazine and Henry said sadly, "It seemed easier on the kids not to tell the truth, but the truth of it was that I wasn't telling the truth."

"It seemed to be a normal life to me," he reminisces about those days with his family in Connecticut. "But no one comes equipped with bifocal hindsight." Almost from the start, the public roles and private lives of the family were at catastrophic odds. John Steinbeck stated what the kids only felt, "Henry is a man reaching but unreachable, gentle but capable of sudden wild and dangerous violence. His face is a picture of opposites in conflict."

Jane adored her father. She recalls, "I spent half of my young life wanting to be a boy because I wanted to be like my father." Peter was always rebellious, his father recalls, "We overworried about him."

After their mother's death the children were sent to a series of schools, and Hank's nightly *tour de force* in *Mr. Roberts* continued until October 28, 1950, when he left the show because of a knee operation. He had played more than a thousand performances of *Mr. Roberts,* never missing a curtain. He went on the road, adding another three hundred performances to the play and finally the *Reluctant* went into dry dock in Los Angeles in August, 1951.

Less than a year after Frances' death, Henry married Susan Blanchard, stepdaughter of Oscar Hammerstein II. During their honeymoon, Peter, ten, aimed a gun at his stomach and pulled the trigger. The slug went through his liver. The Coast Guard summoned Fonda back from St. John's in the Virgin Islands, away from the family and the telephone.

The chronicles of the Fonda children are their own story, too complicated for this brief look at the Fonda career. Perhaps Jane explained their problems best when she wearily told of Daddy's objections to her bare-foot life in St. Tropez several years later when she shacked up with French director Roger Vadim. "Father was living in Malibu and the only difference was that he'd send his chicks home at night. His duplicity blew our minds."

Through it all, the children's rebellion, when they were mere babes, their escapades as young adults, Fonda retained a visible worn exterior. He learned parenthood the hard way, and today the Fondas seem a family that has mastered the magic of adjusting to each other's individuality—an accomplishment that has been long and, in many respects, tortuous for all three, Henry, Jane and Peter.

* * *

By all the rules of the business, Hank should have cashed in on his national popularity directly after *Mr. Roberts* and made a film—any movie.

41

But he didn't. Having found his freedom, Hank appeared determined to enjoy it. So he chose to stay in the theatre, following *Roberts* with *Point of No Return,* Paul Osborne's adaptation of J.P. Marquand's novel of a power struggle in big business which played a respectable number of performances in New York before going on the road.

In 1954, there came the *Caine Mutiny Court Martial,* an adaptation of the Herman Wouk novel in which Fonda played Lieutenant Greenwald, assigned to defend the mutineers against Captain Queeg. To many, this was the performance of his career—choosing between it and Mr. Roberts became a matter of personal taste, so finely had Fonda drawn both characterizations.

By 1955 when Warners got around to filming *Mr. Roberts* the bankers had as much control of the movie business as the old tycoons ever did. They felt Fonda had been away from the screen too long to repeat his stage success. It seems incredible— but then remember what happened a few years later when Audrey Hepburn, not Julie Andrews, fell flat on her long, pointed nose in *My Fair Lady.* John Ford, the director, insisted on Hank. Fonda returned to Hollywood after an absence of seven years, took over his old cargo ship, and sailed it again into boxoffice and artistic riches. Artistic in the movie sense; to purists it didn't compare to the play.

Mervyn LeRoy took over the direction when John Ford became ill, but there was already trouble aboard. Fonda resented the intrusion of physical comedy; in short, he sought to reject the hokum but, of course, he was no match for the Hollywood dictators. Besides bringing Fonda back to the screen *Mr. Roberts* reminded everyone what a beautiful movie actor William Powell had been. The handsome veteran hauled himself up from Palm Springs retirement to play the part of the ship's bibulous "Doc" and quietly hooked every scene he appeared in.

1956 brought Fonda, Susan Blanchard Fonda, Peter and Jane to Rome where Hank had been signed for the three and a half million dollar production of *War and Peace* for the role of Pierre. Audrey Hepburn (the first actress to ask and get a half million dollars for a picture) had been signed for Natasha and her husband, Mel Ferrer, was cast as Andre. King Vidor was the director and other players in the international company were Vittorio Gassman, John Mills, Oscar Homolka, Helmut Dantine, Herbert Lom and Anita Ekberg. I was the unit publicity man for the picture for a period of several months—several months longer than I should have been.

As far as I was concerned the Tolstoy caper was all war and no peace and this eventually proved to be the fate of Henry Fonda as well. He battled with the producer about his interpretation of the role and with Vidor who wrote harshly about his experiences with Hank. I wasn't around when that particular drama took place. My whole experience with Fonda was pleasant, professional but somewhat shaky and fleeting—although Fonda never knew it. Because a press agent's job is to protect the production no matter how messy it becomes I couldn't confide to one of the stars that I might be ducking out at any moment.

So I went through motions, greeting the Fondas when they arrived and awed by the sheer physical glory of the family—Henry's handsomeness and the fragile beauty of Susan Blanchard. The Fonda children were unbelievably lovely.

We had a press contingent on hand and Fonda, I was relieved to note, was going to be an easy man to handle. He took it all in stride, posed for the photographers, gave every question a thoughtful answer and had that capacity to make each newspaperman believe, for a brief instant, that he was the most important person in Fonda's life. That's a key to good public relations and possibly may explain why Fonda has always enjoyed a good reputation with newspapermen.

When I looked at Fonda more closely in the lovely villa, high on a hill, that Hollywood had rented, I had time to notice an expression that wouldn't leave him. He looked to be a sad and worried man—and eventually I learned he was. My instincts told me I should give Hank a lot of time, keep him as busy as I could with the press, whip up interviews, get the TV people in to see him while he was going through costume fittings and starting work. He was wonderful. He cooperated like a little kid. I brought Margaret Truman to the set and a picture of Hank and the ex-president's lovely daughter played around the world. He was getting good publicity. The Italian press enjoyed him as, indeed, did I.

I was as surprised as any of the newspapermen on the Cinecitta beat, the Italians and foreign press alike, when the news front paged that Susan Blanchard Fonda had left Rome within a month or so of their arrival. It was predicted that the Fonda marriage had ended.

If any movie troupe in the world needed comedy relief it was *War and Peace,* what with Audrey Hepburn busying herself with every detail, Mel Ferrer making a lot of noise, Hank brooding about his private life, and King Vidor rewriting the script every night. Fortunately we had Anita Ekberg, the blonde Amazon, who had a short but important role that didn't keep her from visiting the set every day wearing stretch pants and low-cut blouses that show-cased their contents like an ice-cream cone with a double-dip crammed on top. As one British actor said, "I really don't know what the etiquette is in this case. Should I just stare at them as I want to—or pretend that they don't exist?" Anita once nudged me, "You know, there's an electrician who keeps staring at me. It makes me nervous." I asked her who he was. "I don't want to point him out," she answered. "It's that dark looking man over there." At the other end of the set I saw a group of dark-haired Italian crew members, wondering, like the British actor, what was the etiquette?

With the departure of Mrs. Fonda, Anita no longer worried about the leering dark eyes of Italian electricians. She took Hank firmly in tow— and the quiet, taciturn man suddenly became a bundle of charm, as bewildered, astonished and fascinated by Anita as everyone else. She took complete charge of the man, cooking for him, bringing his lunch every day, warming it up on an electric stove she improvised on the set. Hank was overwhelmed.

A newspaper correspondent whose publisher was coming to town asked, as a personal request, for me to put on a good show for his benefit. I did, a guided tour of the astonishing *War and Peace* sets, the exquisite detailed reproduction of the Kremlin, a cordial visit to Audrey Hepburn's dressing room where she gave the party plenty of time and finally lunch with Henry Fonda. After depositing the group at the Cinecitta commissary I drove to Henry's dressing room. He looked at me hopelessly, "Do you mind if I bring Anita along." "Of course not," I lied, and drove to lunch.

It became Anita's party as she monopolized the conversation with a detailed account of her adventures in Rome, concentrating especially on her difficulties with the management of the Grand Hotel where she had been quartered on her arrival. The desk apparently took a dim view of Anita's entertaining habits, especially of the gentlemen callers who arrived late and stayed late. Anita explained vividly, "I told them that this was my home away from home, and I intended living as I always had. And my gentlemen friends were welcome at any time of the day or night."

For a press agent it was rough going; for Henry, too. He mumbled through the meal and tried twice to take over the conversation, getting nowhere. Next day I called the publisher's wife and started

In his seventies, Fonda has taken to the stage in a memorable one-man show, "Clarence Darrow."

to apologize. "Sorry? Don't be ridiculous. My husband had the best time ever since we left New York. He thinks you're the greatest—parlaying all that beautiful production, then Hepburn, Fonda and that fabulous Ekberg. He's like a kid rolling his hoop down the Veneto."

Some weeks later I received a letter from New York thanking me "for making them at home in their home away from home."

Had the Fonda children not been whisked away to boarding schools after the departure of their stepmother and had they enjoyed more of the earthy practical influence of Anita around the house, theirs might have been an entirely different story. At any rate, the reign of Anita as Hank's "lady" was brief. His role neared completion at about the same time that I finally decided it was best to call it quits and leave the quarrelsome members of the *War and Peace* company to their own devices. I went off to Spain to join another movie where, at least, the quarrels would be new and involved different personalities.

* * *

With *War and Peace,* Fonda began what you would call the "distinguished actor" phase of his career. Sometimes he enjoyed top billing; often, he costarred. Now the roles that came his way were his own choices, and there was no longer the studio to blame for things like his episode as Don Ameche's stooge in the invention of the telephone. Generally, Fonda proved a wise judge of his own capacities, and the list of credits rolled on, *Advise and Consent, The Wrong Man* (with Alfred Hitchcock), *The Longest Day* (Darryl Zanuck's all star epic of D-Day), *How the West Was Won* (costarring again with James Stewart under John Ford's direction), *The Best Man* and *12 Angry Men,* which he literally pushed into production. It was a behind-the-scenes story of a jury at a murder trial with Fonda cast as the lone voice against the conviction. He ultimately finds the link that fits the puzzle together and proves the man innocent.

In 1962, Fonda and Olivia de Havilland gave the performances of their careers on a Broadway stage in *A Gift of Time,* a study of a man dying of cancer and aware of it, written with insight and sensitivity by Garson Kanin. It was a beautiful performance and you could hear the stars' heartbeats and feel them counting breaths as they timed their work. The newspaper strike dimmed it out of its existence, but the few who saw it remember *A Gift of Time* and its players as something rare and touching in the theatre.

Fonda was sixty-nine and there would seem no more peaks for him to climb. He had been at the crest of all the mountains—stage, screen and television. In his sixties he'd done the revivals he wanted to do, like *Our Town* and he appeared in community theatres.

Most of the Fonda news seemed to center around his children. Jane became the sexual rebel, triumphantly denouncing marriage, appearing topless and occasionally, bottomless, in films. "Daughter? I don't have a daughter," Fonda once said during her Francophile period when she was under the influence of Roger Vadim. He refused to see some of her pictures and failed to attend her wedding.

While Jane had cornered sex on the screen, Peter took over violence. His big role was the vicious cyclist in *The Wild Angels* and the biggest poster seller of the year was Fonda on a chopper. Peter married and presented his father with his first two grandchildren. Meantime Hank had married and divorced Afdera Franchetti, after the Blanchard marriage ended. In 1965 Fonda married Shirlee Adams, a former airline stewardess.

But Peter's placid married life had not turned him away from the world of free association. On occasion, the subject turned to drugs, which led him into court in Los Angeles with his father at his side. Said Hank, "I'm here to give moral support and any other support to my son." The case was dismissed but, according to Fonda, "it shook Peter up real good and it should have."

Today the Fondas have put most of their difficulties behind them and Henry has tried to see his children on their terms—not his. He realizes now that he was always a rebel. How could they be otherwise? He resented bitterly the FBI persecution of his daughter and assumes, probably correctly, that his own liberal political tendencies were as much responsible as Jane's uninhibited behavior in public, her candid conversations with the press and overt political activity in the causes she believed in. Fonda had never hesitated to define his political leanings, definitely liberal, a

McGovern supporter in the last election and his interest in *Grapes of Wrath* a half century ago was not simply an actor's dream but an attempt to participate in a social document that belonged to the time.

Fonda today is enormously proud of Jane and Peter. Jane became the family's first Oscar winner, and Peter continues to act and produce.

So what was left for old Hank but to enter his seventies with the toughest theatrical creation possible—a one man show. He'd already experienced the challenge—in poetry and literature readings he'd done at infrequent intervals before. But in choosing Clarence Darrow as his subject and character, Fonda was biting off a large piece of controversial history and complicated theatre.

Fonda said that he fell in love with Darrow when he read the script and that, oddly, he had known very little about the fabled liberal lawyer whose cases wrote legal history—both his victories and his losses. "I was in college," said Fonda, "during the Loeb-Leopold trial involving the two college youths who murdered a fourteen-year-old boy for thrills. So I was aware there was a man named Clarence Darrow, a lawyer. But that was all I ever really remember."

As Fonda researched the material put at his disposal by Irving Stone, one of Darrow's biographers, he got closer and closer to the grand old man of the courts with his boundless capacity for feeling the other man's grief.

Putting the show together and playing it was anything but easy. Eventually Fonda summoned his old friend, John Houseman, to assist in reconstructing the scenes and in the direction. By the time Fonda as *Darrow* arrived in New York, after a fantastic series of tryouts, it was sold out before it even opened. Then, just a few nights before its limited engagement was to end, the news came that Fonda had been hospitalized with a heart attack.

"But it wasn't a heart attack or heart failure," the actor said later, explaining that while walking the street he felt "out of breath." Having just gone through a physical examination, at first he ignored the symptoms, then went to a doctor who said, 'No wonder you're out of breath. You're fibrillating.' That means your heart is going out of rhythm. It's not something that makes you fall down and die."

Equipped with a pacemaker, Fonda returned to *Darrow,* toured the country with it and filmed it for television. He intends reviving it for the rest of life.

"Darrow," he said, "was the most rewarding thing that ever happened to me in a long life." "Nothing says that 'Mister Roberts' or 'Grapes of Wrath' has to happen to you. I've been lucky. To approach 70 (his birthday is May 16) and have this happen to me. At this age, some actors begin to coast. If they're not retired, then they do less work, or they take things they shouldn't take."

Many of his contemporaries would act more, Mr. Fonda said, if the roles were available. "They're not writing plays for older men. I'm too old to be a gunslinger anymore. Every now and then there are grandpa parts."

"I had long runs in *Mister Roberts, Point of No Return* and *The Caine Mutiny Court Martial.* I know that in *Roberts*—after four years—it was better the last night. I enjoy the extra challenge of a long run. By God, you must make it fresh for every audience. If it becomes mechanical, you should change your business, or at least get the hell out of the play. I'll do a play as long as they come to see it. I feel it growing in me with *Darrow.* I can feel more security on stage. I'm filling the 'suit' a little more."

"What I get out of acting is worth more than any money. I'm happiest and most relaxed when I'm onstage. I look forward to it. It's terribly important to me to be good."

PART TWO

James Stewart

"*The audience will tell me when it's time to quit.
I love making movies. I've never felt it was a
boring job. It's not only fun but exciting to me,*"
Jimmy has said many times. "*I feel that I've
accomplished something when people come up to
me and say, 'I don't know if it means anything to
you, but you have given me and my family a great
deal of enjoyment over the years.'*"

*O*nce he's put down that "Jimmy Stewart is one of the finest actors alive," the writer might easily assume that his job was done. He's said it all in the light of looking at Stewart today, age sixty-seven, rich, married to the same woman for more than forty years, proud of his family, a respected member of the establishment. Cautious and conservative, only the familiarity of his face, the still lean lanky frame, blue eyes hidden now behind wrinkles and snow-white but still unruly hair distinguish him from any other self-made millionaire able to look back upon his life with smug satisfaction.

But it's not quite that simple. Stewart is a vastly more complicated man than his image suggests, and the clue lies with his occupation—actor. No man who has earned his livelihood as an actor, good, bad or indifferent can ever be described as "simple"—much less one whose half a century before the public has carried an aura of distinction and consistency that automatically entitles him to a niche in Hollywood's Hall of Giants.

Another clue lies in the name the world knows him by—"Jimmy." True, James Stewart has appeared on marquees and on movie titles—but that has been merely a concession to tradition. Stewart has been "Jimmy" to two generations of movie-goers for so long that it is unlikely he'd even respond to his given name. You earn that sort of affection over a long period of time and no one who has ever enjoyed it takes it lightly. Certainly not Jimmy Stewart who never lost sight of the fact that his career began and grew because, right from the beginning, audiences liked him. "Being liked" has been the keystone of Jimmy's craft, the secret of his art. To assume that it all happened naturally and easily is to underestimate an extraordinary personality in motion picture history. Beyond experiencing the "breaks" that belong in the early career of every successful actor, Stewart's enduring success is the product of giant-sized talent combined with careful planning. Even if a career in the theatre never occurred to him until after he entered college and found his original interest in architecture drifting toward acting.

James Maitland Stewart was born in Indiana, Pennsylvania, on May 20, 1908, the son of Alexander and Elizabeth Stewart. His Scotch-Irish father was the owner of a thriving hardware store. As a boy, Jim's hobbies were building wood-and-baling-wire versions of airplanes and playing an accordion which his father had taken in as credit from a customer. After two years of high school in his home town, Jimmy went to Mercenberg Academy and then on to Princeton as a freshman. As a college freshman he started out to major in electrical engineering but when a professor told him he was hopeless, Jimmy quietly shrugged his shoulders, turned to art and then to architecture.

For a lark, during his sophomore year, he played his accordion in a tryout of Princeton's famous Triangle Club Show. To his surprise, he made the cast. "That show changed my life," Jimmy said afterward, "because I felt what it was like to be applauded." There was nothing in his background to prepare himself for the experience. Like most kids of his generation, Jimmy had seen stock companies and had enjoyed silent movies, but, unlike some young hopefuls, he'd seldom identified himself with the heroes he saw either on the stage or the screen.

When he was graduated from Princeton in 1932 with a bachelor of science degree in architecture his parents had visions of a Frank Lloyd Wright. Jimmy, not anxious to disappoint them, said nothing. He'd already learned a character trait that has stayed with him throughout his life, to keep his own counsel until the time came to speak up.

His best friend at college was Joshua Logan, already introduced in these pages as the young man who became a famous director and played a large part in the career of Henry Fonda. He assumed the same role in the life of Jimmy Stewart and, for that matter, in the destinies of a number of people, then and later, as he progressed to become one of Broadway's most distinguished directors. Logan's influence has been enormous.

In the Triangle Show, the feature best remembered was the chorus line of "boys dressed up as girls." Princeton wasn't co-ed and, as at most male colleges, girls seldom played parts in the theatrical production. Jimmy wasn't aware of it, but his first performance on the stage caught the eye of a professional, Bill Grady, then a talent scout for Metro-Goldwyn-Mayer. Grady later moved to Hollywood where he became the studio's casting director and served as surrogate father for years to bit players, character people and stars alike. He noted Stewart, Grady said later, "because he was the only boy who didn't ham it up." That must have been a pretty difficult accomplishment in view of Jimmy's height, six feet, three inches. But he was a skinny kid, with a baby face and probably looked stunning in drag. Put that together with an attempt to play a part and Grady's comment makes sense.

Because of the depression there were few calls for the talents of untried architects, so Jimmy found it easier to drift to New York, with his pal, Joshua Logan, where they both began to hustle roles in Broadway and in stock. He was able to join a stock company in Falmouth, Massachusetts, where a play called *Good-by Again* enjoyed a tryout. Its star was the late Osgood Perkins, father of Tony Perkins. Jimmy played the three-line role of chauffeur and was on the stage only two minutes. Still he managed to turn that brief period into a laugh. The critics noticed him.

Coming to New York in 1932 Jimmy and his roommate, Henry Fonda, began the lean years of making the agents' rounds and eating catsup sandwiches at the Automat. Humphrey Bogart later recalled that sometimes a group of actors would dash into the Automat where one of them, usually Jimmy, would start screaming and moaning, "I'm hungry. I'm dying. I haven't eaten for a week." Then he'd fall into a faint. Sympathetic customers would either give up part of their meals or offer money to the tall, emaciated looking young man and the actors would enjoy a feast. Bogart said, "I swear Stewart was such a good actor he could even make his eyes bulge out like a madman and turn his complexion grey." Stewart recalls, "Sometimes Hank and I were lucky to have fifteen cents between us."

But you couldn't miss either Fonda or Stewart as they made the Broadway haunts. Their height made them stand out in a crowd, and both young men literally bounced with energy, good humor and a sense of the ridiculous that contrasted with the stark realities of the time. They were broke— but happy broke. Their optimism was infectious.

They got noticed, and that was important when so much talented competition existed even for the smallest part in the Broadway theatre. Although the depression was at its depth, the theatre was never finer than in the thirties. Playwrights were exploring new avenues of expression, the Theatre Guild and Group Theatre were developing subscription audiences, a feat in itself. Admission prices were low and fragile plays achieved respectable runs, literally impossible today when the finest works disappear from the boards within a pair of performances, knocked out by outrageous operating costs.

They wouldn't even consider a play by like *Yellow Jack* today, a dramatization of Walter Reed's fight against yellow fever which gave Jimmy his second Broadway opportunity after repeating his chauffeur bit in *Good-by Again*. It called for a large cast, a big production and virtually every part, large or small, was a good one. Jimmy played Sergeant O'Hara, an idealistic soldier guinea pig and Critic Robert Garland wrote: "*Yellow Jack* might have been a more impressive spectacle had the other actors taken their cue from Mr. Stewart." Evidently they did, for the play was a success of sorts.

Then there was praise for Jimmy as Teddy Parish, a boy embittered by his mother's infidelity in *Divided by Three* which came along in 1934. There were a couple of other minor stage appearances by Jimmy in minor plays and to each he brought distinction. He was very much aware of the *scene* in the thirties; the Mecca for most young actors was Hollywood and any kid who got his foot on a Broadway stage realized that at any performance he might be seen by a casting scout. They were invisible Merlins who could transform a nobody into somebody by the simple act of recommending a screen test.

Of the Merlins, none possessed a keener eye than Bill Grady who had been watching young Stewart since his days at Princeton. But Grady waited until Jimmy had appeared on film. He got a part in a two reel comedy produced by Warners at its studio in Long Island, one of the last of its kind to be operated by a major company. Warners did a lot of musical shorts there, featuring Broadway and radio stars like Ruth Etting, Edgar Bergen, Charlie McCarthy and Jane Frohman.

Grady persuaded Metro to pick up Jimmy for the part of a police reporter in *Murder Man* and the studio gave him the typical contract of the era—a six months deal at anything from $75 to $200 a week with options that kept the actor in its fold for seven years with provisions for salary raises. They eventually came to be known as "slave contracts," but in 1935, no one ever went on record as turning one down unless it was a potential starlet who had suddenly found a millionaire husband. Or a young man whose Oklahoma family discovered oil in their backyards. Neither Fonda nor Stewart belonged to that school—they were actors and in the business for whatever it might bring them, three meals a day, a roof over their heads, a chance to express themselves; stardom, maybe. Neither made a big thing of it, but the dream lay tucked away in their hearts. Both had confidence in their abilities.

When Jimmy arrived in Hollywood he moved in with Fonda who was under contract to Walter

63

Wanger at a thousand dollars a week—an unbelievable amount of money. Of his screen debut in *Murder Man* in 1936, Jimmy said later, "I was all hands and feet and didn't know what to do with either."

Jimmy was something of an oddity when he started out, a tall, gawky, slow-speaking leading man at a time when patent-leather handsomeness was cherished. There were many conferences at MGM to decide whether Jimmy was worth his salary. He was not as handsome as Clark Gable; certainly, not like Robert Taylor, who needed years to live down his "beautiful boy" image. Jimmy's bean pole physique, weighing in at one hundred and thirty pounds, was far from beefcake. But Jimmy and Taylor had something in common. The fans discovered them immediately. And when the fan mail for Jimmy started pouring in by the bagful, that decided it. Fans made stars, and Jimmy was in. It lay pretty much within the realm of his own talents to make the success stick.

During his first five years in Hollywood Stewart made twenty-four movies, including Frank Capra's *You Can't Take it With You*, in which he was one of an all-star cast, an Academy Award best picture winner. He did a remake of *Seventh Heaven* and his first Western, *Destry Rides Again*. But it was his role as the idealistic young filibustering Senator in Capra's *Mr. Smith Goes to Washington* that really put Stewart into the star business. The New York Film Critics chose him as the best male actor of 1939. A year later Jimmy won an Oscar for his performance as the reporter

Audiences quickly took a shine to Jimmy when he brought boyish, all-American charm to movies.

in *The Philadelphia Story* opposite Katharine Hepburn.

By the time Jimmy got around to Mr. Smith his style had been clearly defined, the clean-cut, young American, lean, lanky, given to stammering, making improbable gestures to express uncertainty, a master of the double-take, the wry look and surprised hurt. Boyish and shy, every mother knew he could be trusted with her daughter, but the daughters hoped that mama was wrong.

In reviewing *Mr. Smith Goes to Washington,* the *New York Times* wrote: "As Jefferson Smith, James Stewart is a joy for this season, if not forever. He has too many good scenes, but we like to remember the way his voice cracked when he got up and read his bill, and the way he dropped his hat when he met the senior Senator's daughter, and the way he whistled at the Senators when they turned their backs on him in the filibuster."

Jimmy's style had become so fixed and seemed so natural that audiences, very early, decided that Jimmy was a screen personality rather than an actor. That did him an injustice. "When people call me a natural-born actor," he said, "I get mad. I say there's nothing natural about camera lights and forty or fifty people standing around watching you all the time. It's hard. And if I give a natural appearance on the screen, you can be damn well sure I'm working at it."

"I've always been skeptical of people who say they lose themselves in a part. Someone once came up to Spencer Tracy and asked, 'Aren't you tired of always playing Tracy?' Tracy replied, 'What am I supposed to do, play Bogart?' You have to develop a style that suits you and pursue it, not just develop a bag of tricks."

Everything about Jimmy Stewart excited the fan magazines—even if he was as difficult to write about as Hank Fonda. But being an "eligible bachelor" was enough to stir the speculative juices of the gossipy ladies who gushed month after month about Jimmy's new romances. He got around to every eligible girl in town, but legend has it that Jimmy lost his heart to Ginger Rogers. And never recovered when Ginger, although liking Jim a lot, didn't quite feel they were made for each other.

Romantically he was one of Hollywood's enigmas. It was no secret that he held every woman he met in awe, thought that each and every one he came across was something out of this world. Too beautiful to be real. Or too real to have what he wanted in a woman—a dreamlike quality which wouldn't dispel his belief that most women were goddesses.

Said ex-college pal and roommate, Jose Ferrer, "He's the cagiest man I've ever known. He's cagey with cars, with scripts, with women. When he does marry she'll have to talk a very good script."

One of the many girls he escorted during that period of his life remembered, "None of us thought that Jimmy would ever get married. Oh, he was close enough a few times, but somehow, he always seemed to hold back, as if he were waiting for something. Just what, not even Jimmy seemed to know."

The ideal woman?

Jimmy answered that question in straightforward Stewart fashion, "The right woman."

A typical Jimmy Stewart story ran something like this:

"It was Margaret Sullavan's husband, Leland Hayward, who telephoned to Stewart when he was in New York recently. Hayward said: 'A client of mine, Olivia de Havilland, is arriving in New York. She'll be alone. Will you meet her at the plane, take her to the opening of *Gone With the Wind* and show her New York?'

"Stewart had read in this column that Olivia had expressed a desire to meet him. But he wouldn't dare telephone her, after the item was printed. He said it would be embarrassing to both. Therefore, he was pleased to obey Hayward's instructions. They have been seeing each other since.

"He is shy with girls. It is this shyness that makes Hollywood actresses believe he is different.

"He is almost always chewing gum. He often has to be reminded to toss it away when doing a love scene.

"He lives alone except for the servants, in a simple house in Brentwood. He walks in and throws his clothing anywhere. He lives in typical bachelor fashion. He doesn't own a swimming pool and wouldn't have a house with a pool.

"He still likes to build model planes. He flies his own plane. He just bought a new one. It is geared so that it will travel only 100 miles an hour. He is as slow-moving in the air as he is any other place.

"He doesn't like to write letters, and he doesn't do as much reading as he'd like to. His favorite author is John O'Hara. He is a typical movie fan and goes to the movies often. If he weren't a star himself he'd be stopping the stars and asking them for autographs.

"He amuses himself by playing the accordion. His favorite selection is *Sweet Sue*. He also plays the flute.

"His best friends are Burgess Meredith, Henry Fonda, Franchot Tone and Bill Grady, the casting director at Metro."

* * *

The Stewarts of Pennsylvania were proud of their military record. Grandpa James Maitland Stewart left his little hardware store in Indiana, Pa. to fight for the Union in the Civil War. His son Alexander left the store twice—first during the Spanish-American War and again as a captain during World War I.

And grandson Jimmy, who might have gone into the family hardware business if he hadn't become an actor, tried to enlist immediately after Pearl Harbor. Much to his chagrin and disappointment he was turned down since he was underweight. A steady diet of bread and spaghetti produced the needed ten pounds, and Jimmy finally entered the Army. Already experienced in flying, he was assigned to the Army Air Corps. He resented the coddling and publicity inflicted on him during his first days in service and he went to the top to use personal influence to get treated like everyone else. He had created a spectacular radio appearence shortly after his induction into the service by being chosen to introduce President Roosevelt at a *March of Dimes* rally. It was read with fervor and the usual break in the Stewart voice. Obviously the movie star was being exploited, and the gesture to simmer the brass down after their enthusiasm at having nabbed such a well-known volunteer was typical Stewart—blunt, even brash. It worked.

Winning his wings in August, 1942, he instructed bombardier cadets for a year until he went to Europe as the commander of an Eighth Air Force bomber squadron. He flew twenty-five missions over enemy territory, some of them as commander of a bomber wing. He returned to the United States in September, 1945, with the Air Medal and the Distinguished Flying Cross with oak leaf cluster.

After his return to Hollywood, Stewart insisted that his war experiences be kept out of film publicity. Even his friends never heard of his exploits first person, and over the years Jimmy has chosen to let the record speak for itself.

The first postwar movies he made carried on the stereotype he had created before Pearl Harbor—the role described by one magazine writer as "the decent, homey Mr. Smith." In Frank Capra's *It's a Wonderful Life,* he played a civic-minded man saved from suicide by his guardian angel. Columnists quoted Hank Fonda's quip, "When Jim stops pretending to be young, he'll become a great artist."

When reviewers picked him up in *Magic Town* they said, "Jimmy is still exuding boyish charm in lethal doses." Jimmy wasn't exactly getting the kind of reception suited to an actor of his age and experience, to say nothing of a man who had grown tremendously within himself through his war experiences. He simply had outgrown the days and the world when Mr. Smith could go to Washington and make headlines. The globe had shrunk in size, and the complications involved rubbed off on everybody—including Jimmy Stewart.

Two films in 1948 provided Stewart with much needed successes, a change of pace and the realization by producers that they risked destroying a valuable property by persisting in casting him as a forty-year old version of *Skippy. Call Northside 777* gave Jimmy an opportunity to play a reporter, but this time he was cast as a newshawk who accomplished a lot more than racing through the city room with a pencil in his ear and wearing a hat turned up at the brim.

Based on an actual case, it dealt with a reporter convinced of a convicted man's innocence of a murder charge who digs back in the newspaper files and stubbornly sifts the evidence, interviews the protagonists involved in the case and ultimately clears him. It was a strong movie, told in semi-documentary fashion, and Jimmy was at his persuasive best.

Rope would have to be called both a success and a failure. It was a Hitchcock thriller and ranks among the master's classics, but it stirred little enthusiasm at the boxoffice because of its grisly theme—thrill murder. Adapted from a play by Patrick Hamilton, Hitchcock duplicated the stage atmosphere by confining the action to a single room—always a mistake in film making and Hitchcock knew better. But he was eager to experiment, as always, and hoped confining of the locale to a single space might heighten the drama. Still, *Rope* was interesting because of its subtle note of homosexuality suggested in the script and contained in the performances and characterization of two fine young actors who played the killers, John Dall and Farley Granger.

Notices on *Rope* were mixed, but there was enthusiasm for Hitchcock's skill in cutting the picture, the imaginative use of color and of course, for the performances of Stewart, Granger and Dall.

Jose Ferrer remembers the day Jimmy broke down and told him that he had finally chosen a wife. In typical laconic fashion he described her, "Name's Gloria. Guess you'll like her. Must meet sometime."

The year was 1948, and Jimmy was forty-one. Gloria Hatrich McLean was what her name implied, a glorious woman, about ten years Jimmy's junior, non-professional with two small sons by her previous marriage (Mike and Ronald). (Ronald became a first lieutenant in the Marine Corps and was killed in Vietnam.) Gloria was a warm, outgoing and good-natured person, quite a contrast to her shy, introverted husband. Two years later twin girls, Judy and Kelly, were born of the marriage—and the life of Jimmy Stewart as the perennial bachelor came to an end. Family life admirably suited Jimmy's growing conservative instincts; Gloria, the good-looking divorcee from Larchmont, New York, became one of the most popular wives in Hollywood, an accomplishment that would have won her awards had she chosen a career in politics.

Hollywoodites found her a bright, witty woman with that Eastern flare and polish Westerners envy even if they denigrate it. Gloria managed to overcome that suspicion easily with her openness and quick accommodation to the role of a public person. She didn't mind the family life stories fan magazines swooped down upon her to write and photograph—nor did she freeze when she read things like *How Gloria Caught The Best Catch in Hollywood,* etc. She'd expected change when she married Jimmy and never considered herself intruded upon. That was part of her job.

Jimmy blossomed with marriage, the built-in family that came with it and the birth of their own children, but to co-workers he remained what he'd always been, a loner, not unfriendly, as Walter Brennan went to pains to explain, "but hard to get to know." Brennan who had worked with Jimmy on several pictures said, "It just seemed that he was always bogged down in thought."

This inability to communicate, of course, has played a large part in the Stewart screen personality, the nasal, tongue-tied drawl and the "Uuh... uuh" pauses that follow.

Jimmy's hesitancy about spitting out words is

as natural in conversation as it is projected on the screen. "I've never been able to organize my thoughts too well," he once told an interviewer. "I seem to have to think everything through before it comes out."

This sometimes has been embarrassing, as Jimmy readily concedes. He once invited Charles Lindbergh to dinner before he played Lindy in *The Spirit of St. Louis*. Of course, Lindbergh had been one of Jimmy's long-time idols.

"I invited Lindbergh to a restaurant a few days before the start of the picture so I could study him at close range. I wanted to discuss his personal memories of the flight. We sat down, ordered dinner, and almost finished it in silence. I don't know what he thought when we got up to leave, but I'll be damned if I could think of anything to say."

This inability to communicate has given the impression of Jimmy Stewart, the loner. On the set of a picture he generally stays off by himself. He's not an easy mark for saccharine comradeship. His penetrating blue eyes and his towering height can keep even the most formidable gladhander at a distance. Still, he's not cranky about fans. He cheerily signs autographs and feigns a smile, but doesn't engage in easy banter when crowds collect around him as he travels outside Hollywood. With his height and long legs, Jimmy finds it easy to keep moving; unlike many stars caught in the same position, he's never allowed himself to get trapped in a crowd.

* * *

74

After the war, Jimmy hit a different pace, playing roles in slick, big-time Westerns.

Howard Thompson, in his series of illustrated portraits of major film stars, does a stunning job of telling how it worked in his description of one of Jimmy's best pictures, *The Stratton Story*. It was made in 1948 and coincided at its release with Jimmy's marriage. Wrote Thompson: "The film was tasteful, heart-tugging drama, from a beautifully understated screen play by Douglas Morrow and Guy Trosper. Equally imaginative and honest was the direction of Sam Wood, who saw to it that the picture was touching but never treacly. As the brave, gritty protagonist surmounting the loss of a leg, Stewart was superb, fully projecting the despair and hopelessness of a baseball-diamond athlete abruptly rendered 'half a man' yet manfully grappling for emotional strength to face up to the reality of his dilemma.

"In one of the memorable dramatic moments of Hollywood films about sports figures (comparable to Gary Cooper's stadium farewell, as Lou Gehrig, in *Pride of the Yankees*), Stewart is first shown walking with his new wooden leg. We see him, grimly surrendering pride and mastering shame, as he slowly stands, unaided, and carefully teeters across his yard at home, back to the camera, grasping the tiny fingers of his small son who is just learning to walk for the first time. The two figures, tall and short, inch into the background, unforgettably.

"Excellent performances also came from June Allyson as Stratton's wife, Frank Morgan and Agnes Moorehead. Miss Allyson reportedly made off with the front doorknob of the studio's Stratton home facade as a fond souvenir of the movie.

"Of the three films in which Stewart portrayed famous Americans, the Stratton drama was the most effective."

Unlike many alumni of the old studio system, Jimmy feels no animosity to the production assembly line or the men who invented it. He told interviewers, when he came to TV, that "The executives were not power-mad tyrants. Producers and directors frequently had freedom. And actors were treated well. You worked all the time, fifty-two weeks a year. They protected you... took care of your publicity."

But, then, Metro had treated Stewart fairly well, even if they did scoot him over to an independent studio to make *Pot O' Gold,* based on a radio show produced by Elliott Roosevelt. It was notable only in that Mrs. Roosevelt visited Hollywood, charming everyone with her graciousness. One secretary on the lot fainted dead away when the president's wife walked into her office, extended a hand and said, "Good morning, Miss Smith." Paulette Goddard was Jimmy's leading lady and *Pot O' Gold* was the movie which decided her to quit movies and collect jewels instead of film credits.

Apart from this, Jimmy had very little to complain about. MGM was certainly top drawer; unlike Hank Fonda he wasn't mortgaged to a mediocrity like Walter Wanger nor was he second choice at 20th Century-Fox where the pick of top male roles went to Tyrone Power. Fox suffered a bad reputation for star building while Metro succeeded with shrewd judgment and adroit exploitation.

On the other hand, after returning from service,

Jimmy finished his Metro contract in short order and chose to handle his own career and enjoy the freedom of choice that went with it. He was the first star to ask a percentage as the price of his services. The step was deliberate and well calculated, "cagey" as Jose Ferrer had said. Stewart could foresee the change that would shock Hollywood in the fifties, diminish its importance in the sixties and reduce the old studios to nostalgic landmarks in the seventies, sealed away in memory under the steel and cement of skyscrapers and freeways built on land once housing the workshops of the greatest collection of talent in the world.

Lean, lanky "aw shucks" Jimmy Stewart who came to Hollywood as a shy, tongue-tied young leading man, awed by women, but fairly confident of his talent, seemed an unlikely candidate for the rarified atmosphere of the millionaire. But Jimmy had a great deal going for him. He aged gracefully and handsomely. With age and maturity there came stronger, meatier parts, far different from the innocents of his early days.

With the record on the books, it is pretty clear these days that Jimmy was the cleverest of the four giants—at least in turning up the right card at the right time. He wasn't possessed of Hank's artistic zeal; he could never have been as full of himself as John Wayne and he bore no resemblence to Gary Cooper who never wanted to forget that he'd once been a sex symbol, even if it involved silicone plastic surgery to restore his weatherbeaten face in Coop's declining years.

Jimmy always had a reputation for keeping his

cool, and nothing substantiated the impression more deeply than the ease with which he glided through the fifties, deftly moving into roles that enriched his talent. He renewed his association with Hitchcock in *Rear Window* and *The Man Who Knew Too Much.* He played comedies like *Bell, Book and Candle,* tangled with crime in *Anatomy of a Murder* and dabbled in a phase of movie making Jimmy knew could be his old-age annuity—westerns. He displayed a tough-minded, very physical Jimmy Stewart in *Bend of the River, Winchester 73,* and several others. He liked what he had seen of Westerns before the war in *Destry Rides Again,* and he was pleased to find that his flair for outdoor drama had been enhanced with the years.

Then there was *Harvey.*

Harvey was the lone success of Mary C. Chase, a midwestern playwright who had created as her title character a six-foot, three-and-a-half inch rabbit, visible only to Elwood O. Dowd. The rabbit accompanies Elwood, a whimsical drunk, wherever he goes and the play centers around the efforts of his sisters to put Elwood away where "he can be taken care of." By play's end, the genial tippler has convinced everyone that Harvey is real—including the attendant who comes prepared to remove Elwood physically to a "rest home" if necessary.

Harvey won a Pulitzer Prize for Mary Chase, made a fortune for producer Brock Pemberton and must have earned the late Antoinette Perry, his wife, some special saintly mansion in the hereafter for prevailing upon Pemberton to buy the play and to cast one of the most troublesome actors in the American theatre in the title role. He was Frank Fay, whose turbulent career as a brilliant vaudeville comedian had earned him a reputation as a nasty drunk, a bigot, a no show performer, a husband who exploited his wife, Barbara Stanwyck, in order to return as a headliner to the Mecca of all vaudevillians, New York's Palace theatre. He was famed for insulting audiences and walking out on them and only Al Jolson outclassed him in jealousy of other performers. On Broadway Pemberton, heretofore respected as a cautious, conscientious producer, was assumed to have suddenly lost his mind. *Sonuvabitch* was the mildest of adjectives used to warn Pemberton against hiring Fay.

Several years before *Harvey*, Fay, inexplicably, had tossed off a drink at the Lambs Club bar and said to no one in particular, "This is it. I've had it." He never touched another drop. Then, as though leprechauns were writing the script, the Fay stories began. He had embraced God, become a daily communicant at St. Patrick's and up and down Fifth Avenue, between the Lambs and the Cathedral, he gave away dollar bills to worthy actors—and even unworthy ones. Fay, the religious; Fay, the dispenser of largess, like *Harvey*, was never quite believed. No one had ever really seen it all happen. True, no one saw him drinking either, but anyone who had suffered Fay's sarcastic barbs, which included almost all the Broadway crowd, couldn't imagine him staying sober long enough to rehearse a play much less show up for opening night. What work he'd gotten in recent years had been in second-rate clubs run by hoods who knew he could still give a good show or kindly theatre tycoons like Sherril Corwin in California who remembered him from better days.

For Frank Fay, *Harvey* became a personal triumph; for Antoinette Perry, it was a vindication of faith. For Broadwayites it was a bitter blow as the weeks rolled by and Frank, *Harvey,* the Pembertons and the cast prospered. For months *Harvey* remained the hottest ticket in town, eventually enjoying a record run and fathering national companies headed by Joe E. Brown and Bert Wheeler.

The "get Fay" contingent maintained he reverted to type toward the end of the run, milking the laughs and ad-libbing lines from his old vaudeville act. Cast members maintained otherwise—that Fay was so set and legitimate in the part that replacement actors never even rehearsed with him but with the stage manager who said, "On this line, Fay will be in this position and react to your line." "I couldn't believe it," said a veteran who'd taken over for Josephine Hull. "I'd never had such an experience but, just as the stage manager promised, there was Fay at precisely the right spot, and I never felt more comfortable playing a new part in my life."

Stewart was interested in *Harvey* from the beginning, and it seemed a made-to-measure movie vehicle for him. Invited to replace Fay he came to New York during the star's summer vacation and performed Elwood Dowd for six weeks. Jimmy's notices were good, but you couldn't say that New York went wild to see a movie star in the Fay part as, for example, it did when Liza Minelli replaced Gwen Verdon in *Chorus Line,* and sold the house out totally for six weeks within a few hours.

When film rights to *Harvey* were sold, it was wrapped up as a package at Universal-International for Jimmy Stewart with Josephine Hull engaged to play her original role. There were other recruits from the Fay cast, and Jimmy's performance won him an Academy Award nomination. Some say Stewart brought more credibility to the part, a sweetness lacking in Fay's performance. Sweetness was exactly the quality Fay avoided—sweetness, archness and mannerisms. He drew his character from the superb vaudeville monologist he'd once been—so sure of himself that he threw away laughs other comics stumbled over to grab. Fay offered a choice—you could see *Harvey* with him if you wanted—or ignore him. Elwood was your guide to a world where fantasies are more pleasant than life's realities.

In any event, *Harvey* was not the film success it had been on the stage. Perhaps it needed the proscenium and the three-dimensional qualities of live theatre to bring the audience to see, as Elwood did, his six-foot-three rabbit.

Stewart himself admitted being dissatisfied with his conception of Elwood when he returned to New York in 1970 to tackle the role again, this time for a six weeks' engagement with Helen Hayes in

Jimmy was 41 when he married socialite Gloria McLean—a totally happy, enduring union.

the Josephine Hull role at the ANTA theatre. He said, "I think Elwood P. Dowd is much closer to my own age now than it was twenty years ago. I played him a little too dreamily, a little too cute-cute. I don't intend to do that this time."

Stewart didn't and the press was ecstatic. One critic put it this way: "He is offering a class in acting at each performance." Jimmy wasn't aware of his triumph until the following morning. After the opening, the Stewarts quietly went off to their hotel and to bed. Either they weren't aware of the New York tradition of waiting up for the reviews or chose to ignore it.

* * *

In his public relations Jimmy has led a charmed life. He could never complain about the press. They'd treated him fairly and decently. He barely knew what bad publicity was. He neither scampered down alleys at the sight of photographers nor stood still for hours on end while they snapped away the thousands of frames that compose the photographic art. There had always existed an easy rapport between newsmen and the actor. He felt no need for a press agent to monitor his interviews after he'd left the shelter of MGM where the policy was mandatory. When newsmen came to see him, Jimmy usually opened the door himself, making the visitor instantly comfortable.

Writing in the New York *Times,* Judy Klemesrud reported: "Only time and fame and money can bring you that kind of security. He is also secure enough to wear his horn-rimmed glasses, to answer every question without flashing a not-that-one-again grimace (and if anyone has heard them all, he has), and not to order up one of those mammoth carts of eats-and-drinks from Room Service."

In 1959, however, Jimmy made uncharacteristic headlines with, out of the blue, it was announced that Colonel James Stewart, after fourteen years without a promotion, had gotten himself a military star. He was named a Reserve brigadier general. The Air Force proposed him, the President named him and the Senate approved the promotion. What would normally have been a sweet personal moment of triumph evoked a sour taste and widespread controversy over the reasons behind the appointment. How much of the promotion was attributable to his stature as a prominent American personality and how much to fulfilling his duty as a reserve officer? These were the questions other Air Force officers began asking. Lyndon Johnson, then the Democratic majority leader in the Senate, announced that he planned a sweeping investigation of the whole system of military promotions involving the rank of general and admiral. It was an obvious play to his constituents in a Republican administration (Dwight Eisenhower's) and a promotion involving a prominent Republican (Stewart).

The Senate approved the promotion in 1959, reversing an action taken two years earlier when it was blocked by Senator Margaret Chase Smith, a feisty Maine Republican, who pointed out that after his return to civilian life, Colonel Stewart had put in only nine days of training. The period she questioned covered eleven years. She asked how he could qualify for the job of general with a mobilization assignment which in the event of war would make him *Deputy Director of Operations for the Strategic Air Command.*

Senator Smith was always at her best when she took on the whole Senate, so they backed away from the promotion. But a compromise had been worked out. In the two years after Senator Chase protested, Jimmy put in fifteen days of training and his mobilization assignment was downgraded. The Air Force switched his assignment for SAC operations to public relations. In case of war, he will be *Deputy Director of Information in the office of the Secretary of the Air Force.*

If the downgrading and the public furor engineered by Senator Smith was painful, Jimmy gave no indication at the time. His friends thought it was a snide payoff to a man who might have accepted deferment because of his weight. On the opposite side of the coin there were millions of young Americans who worked hard to stay out of the Army, in contrast to Jimmy, who worked hard to join and set a good example. They remember Jimmy as the first major movie star to enlist; they remember his subsequent refusal to capitalize on his war record and his competence as an operations officer.

But the incident *did* rankle him and after it had all died down he admitted that he wished Margaret Smith "hadn't done that thing." He told a couple of interviewers, "I didn't say anything then and I won't now. I'm just trying to do the best I can."

As a reserve officer Stewart's period of active duty represents only a fraction of his military activity. He gives a great deal of time to the Army's recruiting programs, making documentary films and boosting SAC as "our first line of defense." Stewart has often said that he might have chosen military service as a full-time career. Instead the luck of those early days made him an actor.

As far as the public was concerned it was all a tempest in a teapot. They had no trouble in separating Jimmy the actor from Jimmy the general. What he did with his spare time was his business; what he was doing on the screen interested them more.

But that was in 1959—a simpler era when the country had not lived through the Vietnam war, the assassinations of the Kennedy brothers, the murder of Martin Luther King, the attack on Wallace, the Watergate scandal, the resignations of Agnew and Nixon and all the revelations that have followed—disclosures of the duplicity in high places which has reduced political ethics in this country to a shambles. A man like Stewart, capable of commanding an audience, has to expect his share of brickbats—and he's gotten them— since his alignment with the conservative element in Hollywood represented in the public mind by John Wayne.

There is no real reason for anyone to be surprised at Jimmy's political activism during the last ten years. Except that it appears inconsistent with his youth and with his friends of that day, Hank Fonda, Josh Logan, Burgess Meredith and Franchot Tone, all liberals, if in varying degrees. In an interview some years ago, Fonda admitted that lack of common interests had cooled their old friendship—which was a polite way of explaining that being poles apart politically had affected what once had been an easy camaraderie.

But the years, the growth of his personal financial interests, his twenty-seven years' association with the military, had changed Jimmy markedly. He was not, like Gary Cooper, Sam Wood, the director, Ward Bond, Ginger Rogers and others, a charter member of the *Motion Picture Alliance for the Preservation of American Ideals,* the group which stood in the forefront of the Red Witch Hunts of the fifties. Actually, it was formed before the war, a time when Jimmy was better occupied—furthering his reputation as an actor and eligible bachelor. However, in recent years he became a good friend of Wayne's.

As a staunch Republican he was an ardent Nixon supporter and narrated a nine-minute movie on Mrs. Nixon. With Fred MacMurray, another member of the conservative wing of the movie business, he often played golf with the former president. Reportedly, his attitude toward Nixon has changed since his abrupt retirement from the presidency.

But having found his voice, Jimmy is far from reluctant to articulate his views. Indeed he shares with John Wayne a fear that Communists pose a threat to the nation. "I still feel they are a potential danger in show business," he told a *Daily News* interviewer.

Asked about John Wayne's winning of an Academy Award for *True Grit,* a victory that horrified as many people as it pleased. "I think sentiment entered into it, but that performance he gave in *True Grit* matched anything seen on the screen in a long time. Wayne has never lost his respect, love and enthusiasm for the picture business. People are wrong when they say the star system is dead. All you have to do is look at Big Duke and you know that they're wrong.

"When he won I sent Duke a telegram, 'You've been a tremendous asset to the picture business for an awful long time. Last night, you saved the picture business.' "

Even the Duke, not one to underestimate his role in movie history, must have been shaken up by that out-size tribute, but behind all that Stewart reserve, there lurks a taste for theatrical hoke. Like the Duke, Jimmy's been around an awful long time—long enough to indulge his fantasies. You don't argue with institutions. You accept them for what they are—giants who've earned the right to be rigid in their ideas, dogmatic, single-minded. And Jimmy Stewart certainly qualifies as an institution. Having him around all these years to know and enjoy, to entertain us on the screen, has been sheer joy. His extreme conservatism may please some, disappoint others, and annoy many, but this is the Jimmy Stewart of his senior years. Who is there to question his right to express what his experiences have impressed on him?

At least Stewart speaks knowledgeably and in the light of deep convictions when he says, "The whole attitude toward the military concerns me very much. There are forces today, and where they come from I don't know—probably both from within and without—that are trying to soil the image of the military.

"This is a very dangerous thing. I spent twenty-seven years in the military and it meant a great deal to me. I know the principles and the standards. I learned it made me a better civilian. It's disturbing to see these forces trying to discredit the military and send it back into the isolation like it was after World War I. I think the structure and base of the military contains some of the finest people in the country today—our professional military men."

* * *

If the sixties marked the emergence of Jimmy Stewart as a voice from the right, the decade also saw him become a larger part of that most American of screen form, the Western. Stories rooted in the history of man's conquest of the West suited his maturity. As Howard Thompson observed: "The aging Stewart was not the still handsome prairie dasher conveyed by Gary Cooper, nor did Stewart have the mercurial bluster of a Burt Lancaster, when this actor elected to straddle a horse, or the born-to-the-saddle hulk of John Wayne. The ultimate effect of the James Stewart who emerges from this latter gallery of

90

Old friends and roommates, Jimmy and Hank Fonda, met in London when both were doing shows.

Westerns is that of a wiry, cautious bean-pole, hat and clothes hanging loosely, with slow and barb-wired talk and eyes that bore through as surely and methodically as acid."

Said Stewart, "I'm old-fashioned. Why be an anti-hero when you can be a hero? I've been told I should do something out of character. I feel, with everybody being an anti-hero, I'm doing something different by remaining a hero."

The Western cycle of Jimmy's career reunited him with John Ford in *The Man Who Shot Liberty Valance* and *How the West Was Won*. The latter was all-star and one of those episodic things with George Marshall and Henry Hathaway also sharing directorial credits.

Jimmy also did a pair of Westerns with his old friend Hank Fonda, moving *Time* magazine to note: "Jimmy Stewart and Henry Fonda are as comfortable together in a screen saddle as they have been in a friendship that goes back to 1932 and summer stock. Now the old cronies have teamed up on *The Cheyenne Social Club,* a wonderful outdated odyssey of bawdy innocence."

The film is populated with more pasteboard characters than you could empty a pair of Colt peacemakers at. There is just not one whore with a heart of gold, but six. There is the starched, parched lawyer feller and the inevitable gang of scabrous villains without a redeeming virtue to their sinister names. The dialogue is beautifully peppered with the buckshot of obscure Old West metaphors. 'I used to be a real cedar-breaker but now I'm just bringing up the dregs.' But the film's sole purpose is to give Stewart and Fonda a chance to weave their well-tuned wiles. The result could win the heart of a Wichita banker.

"In this age of permissiveness, who else but Jimmy Stewart could do a double take, mumble incredulously, 'Do you suppose this is a who...' believable? Stewart has a rich cinematic history of clod-kicking embarrassment before the ladies and he can still say 'ma'am' more effectively than anyone else in the business."

The Stewart-Fonda style in *Social Club* seemed effortless, but it involved considerable pain for Jimmy. On location in Santa Fe his horse Pic, Stewart's mount in at least fifteen pictures, died. Stewart was consoled when Hank painted a meticulous likeness of the gelding.

A deeper tragedy struck when Stewart's stepson was killed in Vietnam. Stewart did his best not to brood, and Fonda tried to keep other conversations going—like recalling the time Fonda went to sleep on a bar and awoke to find that John Wayne had wrapped a boa constrictor around his head.

Looking back on his career, Jimmy sees some similarities between himself and the new anti-heros. "Some of the things I did at that age are not so much different from some of the things Dustin Hoffman does now. I did 'Mr. Smith Goes to Washington' in 1939, and that was anti-establishment and against big government and against the lack of integrity in high places."

But most of today's movies leave him discouraged. "I've always felt the medium was indestructible, that it absolutely requires variety. When I hear some new director with one or two pictures under his belt say that the new day has arrived and the motion picture has found its means of expression and that it's complete realism and a completely frank statement of all the human conditions, and that's all a movie should do, then I disagree with him. I think there should be flexibility in movies."

Jimmy's pretty grateful that his era missed the bare-bottom thing. "I look terrible without any clothes on. I wore tights in a picture called *Ice Follies of 1940* and they thought I looked terrible in those. I was supposed to be a champion ice skater, but I wound up as the back end of a horse. Lew Ayres and I flipped for the position and I lost.

"As an actor I think the variety of roles I have had has been fascinating. I wouldn't pick out one particular kind. Well, if I have to: roles like that in the Neville Shute story, *No Highway in the Sky* or that part I had in Frank Capra's *It's a Wonderful Life*. I thought *Anatomy of a Murder* was a good yarn. And some of the Westerns I've done I have enjoyed very much. And, of course, all the Hitchcock movies.

"I've never had the desire to be in complete control of one of my films, to be producer and director. I've done a little directing, of course; I suppose every actor would like to direct. But it isn't something where you can say, "I have been acting for thirty-eight years, so now I can take up direction!"

With young people of college age of his own to worry about, Jimmy has definite ideas about

94

today's young actors and, of course, he is inclined to compare them with his own generation. "I wish today's kids would laugh a little more," he says. "I wish they wouldn't take themselves as seriously as they do. The younger people I've worked with just don't seem to have fun in their craft. As many of them are completely undisciplined and selfish. They seem to be almost self-conscious in scenes. Oh, I wish there was more humor. When I got started, right in the heart of the depression, the theatre was a bright, gay, lively, enthusiastic place and the young people had *fun*.

"There was tremendous activity up and down Broadway, the Group Theatre, the Theatre Guild— those wonderful Bert Lahr shows and wonderful comedians and wonderful Gershwin music—all in the middle of the blackest part of the depression."

* * *

The small screen of television has not been kind to the older actors and the reason may lie in their zeal for continuing popularity—in some cases, because of economic necessity; in others, because of greed. They seem all to have been drawn to the series style of TV adventure. They are intrigued by the idea of doing twenty or thirty prime time segments of the same character, usually a one-dimensional lawyer, doctor or teacher—and then sitting back for life counting the dividends from daytime re-runs.

The women stars, on the other hand, Bette Davis, Joan Fontaine, Joan Crawford, lean to the

TV-made movies, those hour-long pieces of junk containing either a long part for the star or a cameo. Either way, they grab the money and run, doubtful that beyond its initial screening the TV movie will ever be seen again. It's like playing a week in stock at a good salary.

As Glenn Ford has been lured to the TV tube for a couple of goshawful series, so has James Stewart. His first cast him as a college professor getting into cute situations with pretty girls and a canned sound track. It was built around the Stewart personality that belonged to the thirties and was as absurd as it was banal and boring.

That didn't last long and Stewart tried again— turning up in a series called *Hawkins*—playing a nationally known criminal lawyer from West Virginia. 1973 was a big season for lawyers on the boob tube and while Jimmy's *Hawkins* was more interesting than most, played with his usual meticulousness, it fared only moderately well in the ratings. Eventually it disappeared and today Jimmy's TV future seems doubtful. The medium itself is going to have to come up with some new techniques to make full use of the hundreds of older, still popular and damn it, still fine over-fifty-five actors around.

Now, the *Benjamin Franklin* series was an example of what could be done—despite writing that would barely have done justice to an eighth grade composition class. It employed Eddie Albert, Richard Widmark and Melvyn Douglas to portray Franklin at three different ages of his long life. It marked a milestone in imaginative casting and rated an E. for effort—even if the shows themselves put audiences to sleep.

As *Hawkins,* Jimmy wandered through a series of complicated plots, usually involving murder and the series leaned heavily on shock value for its opening show—dealing with homosexuality, bisexuality, hustling, a hotel catering exclusively to males. It was called *Murder in Movieland* and the whole thing was so trite and absurd that it failed even to provoke the wrath of the Gay Liberation pickets.

Hawkins got into less complicated plots eventually, but they were always liberally laced with sex and when TV monkeys around with sex, so much is evaded that it would be better if they left it in the bedroom where it belongs. Bette Davis said it all years ago when she took her first look at the little screen and said, "It's great. It will revolutionize the business. But you'll never get sex on that little screen."

How true! You can put people in bed totally naked together and its prurient effect is practically nil on TV. The viewer's attention is distracted by the wrinkles in the sheets. As Jimmy Stewart pointed out, "To satisfy the Hays office, whenever a girl and boy were on the same bed, in whatever position, one of the boy's feet was always on the floor. Yet we made some pretty provocative love scenes." Melvyn Douglas always complained about the Hays office ban on tongue kissing— something he could never understand—since the camera generally photographed kissing scenes in such a way that the audience never really grasped how the kiss was being administered. The actors utilized slight body movements to convey their reactions. Subtle, inoffensive—and effective. Much more so than the two-in-a-bed scenes that TV considers so daring.

* * *

When the people who write about movies get around, as they frequently do, to their think pieces and list the all-time greats of Hollywood (a convenient way to fill up space on Sundays) they lean on the old reliables, Garbo, Paul Muni (who played in about a dozen movies), Chaplin (to represent the silents), John Barrymore (for no reason beyond *Grand Hotel* and *Dr. Jekyll and Mr. Hyde)*, Spencer Tracy (because everyone swore he was great) and maybe James Cagney, a true great who seldom played a role the match of his talents and, of course, Bette Davis.

But they overlook the bread and butter boys like Cary Grant, Clark Gable and Jimmy Stewart—the fellows who made the screen work for them, for their audiences and, God knows, for their producers. Some were rewarded handsomely with rich contracts, pensions—the lot. Yet when Clark Gable closed out his career at MGM, one of the most illustrious in the studio's history, the King dropped by the lot one day to pick up his personal belongings and drove off. There wasn't an executive in sight to wish him godspeed, not even a gold watch to commemorate his twenty-five years of service. Jack Warner literally pushed Bette Davis out the front gate, after having sabotaged her final pictures at his studio.

When Andrew Sarris of the *Village Voice* commented that "James Stewart was the most complete actor-personality in the American cinema," his readers wanted to know what Sarris meant. He chose to answer the question in a fascinating exploration of Stewart's career from start to finish, summing up as follows:

"...it was when Stewart became too old to be fashionable that he became too good to be appreciated. Suddenly his whole career came into focus as one steady stream of moral anguish. Hitchcock brought out the overt madness in him, the voyeurism *(Rear Window),* the vengefulness *(The Man Who Knew Too Much),* the obsessive romanticism *(Vertigo).* Ford brought out the cynic and opportunist in him. Anthony Mann brought out the vulnerable pilgrim in quest of the unknown. That Stewart even had the opportunity to enrich and expand his mythical personality into his sixties and our seventies, is a fortunate accident of film history. But enriched and expanded he has become through the steady pull of his personality which has evolved over four decades from American gangly to American Gothic. If we preserve his seventy-odd films for posterity, he will belong to the ages as a beacon of the moral fervor that once shaped us. In any event, the cumulative effect of all his performances is to transcend acting with being, the noblest and subtlest form of screen acting."

In England an artist of Stewart's stature would

have been rewarded with knighthood. Instead, Stewart has money. The old shyness returns when that subject is brought up. He protests he is not a millionaire, but the evidence proves otherwise. Every time one of his pictures shows up on TV, a piece of the action belongs to him. He has invested wisely in real estate and is, therefore, able to live the life of a country squire. He may set off a few firecrackers now and then with his political attitudes but he could never stir up the animosity that John Wayne provokes. That's not the Stewart way.

Jimmy and Gloria live quietly in their Brentwood house and there is now time for the things Jimmy enjoys—reading and travelling. He isn't retired by any means. "I'll never quit," he has often said, but like his friend, Henry Fonda, he mourns the fact that juicy parts just aren't there for actors his age. Unlike Fonda he lacks the dedication to the stage that has kept his name lighting up marquees at the age of seventy in *Larrow*. He's never had the same dedication to the theatre as Fonda—nor the experience. Playing *Harvey* seems about as far as he was willing to go.

He once said, "I'm probably not as qualified to comment on the theatre as I am on what is going to happen to the movies. But they are linked together very much. It seems to me that the theatre, just like the movies, is indestructible. Audiences may change, and the way of doing theatre and movies and the economic set-up—all that may change. But they are indestructible.

"The audience will tell me when it's time to quit.

I love making movies. I've never felt it was a boring job. It's not only fun but exciting to me. I feel that I've accomplished something when people come up to me and say, 'I don't know if it means anything to you, but you have given me and my family a great deal of enjoyment over the years.' "

For Jimmy Stewart, *that* is rewarding.

PART THREE

John Wayne

Wayne has never been predictable, and now is hardly the time for gypsy seers to peer into his future. Age is the enemy—age and the condition of his health. Although he has bluffed his way through the past decade, the years cannot have been comfortable or reassuring. To count him out is premature—and that's good. Better a snarling, battling curmudgeon like the Duke to have lived with, been angry with—and enjoyed—than one of those actors they end up describing as a man who never did anything wrong.

As a very small boy, I can recall seeing William S. Hart in *The Great Train Robbery*. It was a short feature on a regular children's Saturday matinee program. This must have been in '24 or '25, a decade or so after it was made. However, the film had not yet become historic and I guess it appeared in place of the two-reel comedy that usually made up the program. Silent films hung around a lot longer than movies do today; still *The Great Train Robbery* struck the kids as pretty silly stuff compared to the action stirred up in the feature pictures of the reigning cowboy stars of the time. Tom Mix, Fred Thompson, Buck Jones, Jack Holt and Hoot Gibson were the most popular of a list that included Ken Maynard, Bob Steele (who did serials), young Johnny Mack Brown,

George O'Brien, Harry Carey, Colonel Tim McCoy, and the Farnum Brothers, Dustin and William, who often played outdoor parts. You'd have to include Rin-Tin-Tin as an awesome Western star at the boxoffice and so was Pearl White, the queen of the serials.

No child of the era could avoid having seen them all, but that didn't automatically mean he enjoyed them. I loathed Westerns; their slim stories bored me to death and, of all the stars, only Rin-Tin-Tin aroused my childish enthusiasm. This discrimination was due to relatives who saw no reason to sacrifice their own tastes as they carted me off to the movies week after week! There was a grandmother, who was in love with Thomas Meighan and adored Valentino; an aunt, devoted to Douglas Fairbanks, Theda Bara and Blanche Sweet; and a sister in love with Ramon Novarro and John Barrymore. My mother, who was a vaudevillian, simply sent me into the auditorium from backstage, totally indifferent to whatever was on the screen as she daily ground her way through four shows.

Then there was the elderly woman who took care of me while Mother was on the road. To my mind, she really knew how to entertain a kid. Her idea of "a show" consisted of the late show at Proctor's where, besides five acts of vaudeville, we got the kind of pictures she preferred, Lon Chaney in *Phantom of the Opera*, Lon Chaney in *Hunchback of Notre Dame*, classy crook stories like *Alias Jimmy Valentine* and Lon Chaney in *The Unholy Three*. Those were nights to remember—especially when the manager came out before the unveiling of Chaney's face in *Phantom* to warn those with weak hearts to shield their eyes. Silly man! That's what we'd come to see.

So my taste in silent movies revolved around Lon Chaney, Lon Chaney and Lon Chaney, Chaplin, Jackie Coogan, Charlie Chase, Blanche Sweet and Dolores Del Rio, whose beauty I can still remember in *Ramona*. I recall following the serial *Melting Millions* steadily because it starred William Farnum and dealt with money.

As a half-grown boy I passed a theatre day after day to look at stills of scantily clad women with their skirts way above their knees. That was part of the naughtiness of *The Road to Ruin* which I suppose you could call the *Deep Throat* of its day. *Ruin* was a fabulously successful "for adults only" movie, produced for peanuts, which mopped up for years. The producers had smartly worked out a scheme that would eliminate certain scenes to suit the prejudices of various state censorship boards. New York State had one of the roughest.

When talkies arrived, the American Western went into temporary limbo because microphones were concealed in various positions, behind chairs, in vases, etc. Cameras had to be placed in soundproofed booths because of their whirring noise. I had no reason to miss the Westerns as movies started to sing and dance, enlivened by the world of Busby Berkeley, luscious beauties like Anita Page, Bebe Daniels and fine actors like "Mr." George Arliss and Ronald Colman. Chester Morris scared the daylights out of us in *The Bat* and old friend Lon Chaney checked in with *West of Zanzibar*, his only talking picture. Chaney died shortly after its completion. There were the Marx Brothers, Garbo's husky voice heard for the first time in *Anna Christie*, vivacious Joan Crawford, Kay Frances and Ruth Chatterton—all acting their heads off while Ruby Keeler danced and Dick Powell sang. Who needed Mary Pickford?

Eventually technicians mastered the problem of mobility and the Western returned in grand style—tentatively in *In Old Arizona* with Warner Baxter which turned out a big hit. Then *Cimarron* came along with its sweeping Edna Ferber story and a glorious performance by Richard Dix.

So the Western had not died after all, but like the rest of the movie world, it was seriously affected by the depression. The giants of the sagebrush, Tom Mix and Buck Jones, were on the road appearing in circuses. So was Colonel Tim McCoy. Fred Thompson died at the peak of his career. Bob Steele drifted into character roles as did Jack Holt. Dustin Farnum died and William Farnum, once listed on studio payrolls at ten thousand dollars a week, was picking up peanuts wherever he could find them. Rin-Tin-Tin failed to survive the talkie era. Of the old timers, there remained only George O'Brien and Ken Maynard.

Harry Carey was drummed out of movies after *Trader Horn*, when he took Edwina Booth's side in her suit against MGM charging that her health had been permanently affected by a disease contracted on location in Africa with the adventure film. Eventually Carey returned in character roles, thanks to John Ford.

By the time I arrived in Hollywood as a young newspaperman in the mid-thirties, Westerns were plentiful. The popularity of the double bill required Hollywood to produce an enormous number of movies annually, thus creating the low budget B picture and the quickie Western. Only three small studios carried "oateater" inventory: Columbia, Universal and Paramount. The last did not produce but released the *Hopalong Cassidys* of producer Harry Sherman.

Virtually all the bread-and-butter Westerns were independently produced out of an area surrounding Gower Street and Sunset Boulevard known as Poverty Road. The intersection, called Gower Gulch, centered around the Columbia drug store, a nearby liquor store, a Western-style bar with whiskey at two-bits a shot, and several shops selling Western outfits, holsters, boots, large leather belts and other paraphernalia—all, incidentally, manufactured in New York City and New Jersey.

Small offices, seldom larger than two rooms, store fronts really, identified the various companies operating along Poverty Row—Chesterfield Pictures, Ambassador Pictures, Monogram, Tiffany, Resolute, Beacon, Majestic and Mascot Films. Unlike older companies tied to familiar trademarks, bright Art Deco signatures with intricate designs and lots of chrome shooting stars and rockets identified the various inhabitants of Poverty Row.

The area's nickname told it all. When Tom Mix died in 1937, the era of the millionaire cowboy star ended. Buck Jones had saved his loot but when he worked afterward it was at a fraction of his old salary. The same held true of Ken Maynard. New names were coming up in the Western field and Poverty Row producers were a hard lot to bargain with.

Poverty Row fascinated me and since my first job involved representing a movie trade paper catering to small town and neighborhood exhibitors I covered it extensively, even developing an affection for it. I knew all the producers and picked up extra money by writing their press books. The first story I wrote for the New York *Times* dealt with the wonders of Poverty Row. The double dealing, the production short-cuts, and all the tricks were part of making acceptable movies in six days at budgets seldom exceeding five thousand dollars. Many veterans of old Hollywood, including Carle Laemmlle, are credited with the phrase, but it was Mr. Stern, father of the Stern Brothers, also known as the Alexander Brothers, who said, "A tree is a tree, a rock is a rock, shoot it in Griffith Park." I spent hours with old Mr. Stern and the Alexander Brothers, picking up the lore of the pioneer days in Hollywood and intrigued by the resourcefulness that went into their way of movie making. Knowing the tricks finally gave me a sense of appreciation of the lowly Western.

None of the producers owned anything. To make their films they rented, borrowed or stole— everything from sound stages to livestock, location areas, and costumes for the women. The Gulch cowboys brought their own. Western Electric, owning all the patents on sound equipment, permitted an independent sound company to operate freely in the Gulch, thus avoiding monopoly charges. There were no guilds; writers took what they were offered for a script and at the larger indies, writers' pay seldom exceeded two hundred dollars a week. Directors' salaries ranged between $500 and $750 a week and star salaries seldom went above one thousand—which meant a thousand a picture.

Financing was precarious and depended largely on the good will of distributors, known as States Rights distributors, who handled most of the independents. Since rentals for quickie product ranged between five and ten dollars a day the producer's share of the dollar never produced the cash flow he needed. He remained in a constant state of debt to the States Rights franchise holders for advances. Sometimes an angel would come along or a couple of bold young men, dreaming of becoming, like Columbia, an "independent major" would try to float stock. In the thirties, investors had had it with issues marked "highly speculative." City Marshalls marched in and out of Poverty Row constantly, sealing off "attached property," consisting of vintage typewriters and battered desks barely worth a junkman's visit.

One of the reasons customers today are obliged to meet deposits for telephone service goes back to a case involving a dispute between a Gulch producer whose telephone service was cut off. After paying the arrears, he was told a deposit was necessary before service could be reinstated. The man, a lawyer, proved there was nothing in existing regulations making a deposit mandatory; moreover, a utility could not demand payment for service not yet rendered. They turned on his switchboard promptly as phone company lawyers sat down to get a deposit regulation through the FCC.

Men brash enough to take on monopolies had no trouble slapping people around; not with a depression on. Top names like Esther Ralston, William Farnum, Frances X. Bushman, Hobart Bosworth, H.B. Walthall, Aileen Pringle drifted down to Poverty Row to pick up what used to be pocket money. The Guilds were standing in the wings, and by 1938 the halcyon days of five dollar extras or family and friends playing extra for "fun" were over. The Screen Actors Guild won its first contract.

But the Gulch cowboys still were glad to pick up $25 a day for bit parts and villains could be bought for $200. You never worried about the girl, usually a newcomer, whose salary was a standard two hundred.

Noah Beery, brother of Wallace and a fine actor in his own right, star of *Chu Chin Chow*, a long run musical in New York and London, once accepted a thousand dollars for a single day's work. It lasted about eighteen hours, but Beery didn't complain until he saw the picture. The director had shot Beery in key scenes showing him as the mastermind of a band of outlaws. A hooded double played the rest of the Beery part, reading lines that Beery had made on "wild track."

Quickie producers knew more about dubbing

than the majors. Paramount, for example, sent the beautiful Isa Miranda packing and back to Italy because of her accent. No one thought to dub the excellent actress until her English improved. The studio threw a valuable property and a million dollars down the drain. That could never have happened on Poverty Row.

I remember once being at the Alexander Brothers' office when a call came through late in the afternoon that the generator on location had failed. With the brothers I raced out to the Valley to find the director serenely winding up the day's work with light to spare. He'd lined up all the trucks and cars belonging to the company, placed them in a key position, turned on their headlights and told the cameraman, "Roll 'em."

Indoor fight scenes were always saved for Saturday night, the last day of shooting, when, instead of a dollar for eating money, the boys were given two. That bought a quart of *Old Dynamite* and, even with pulled punches, those oateater fight scenes were something to watch.

My favorite memory of Poverty Row was the weekend I spent watching a set decorator do over a period piece while the costume department whipped up a modern wardrobe for the heroine. In all the standing sets—bar, homestead, outside the general store, inside the general store, bright new signs were pasted advertising a popular brand of chewing gum. On Friday night the producer had pocketed a couple of grand from the gum company to change his picture from period to modern and show the hero opening sticks of gum at every

113

opportunity. This seldom happened on Poverty Row. Worse luck! Payola for the display of products was more common on the big lots. Indie producers survived by skimming their money off the top—grabbing the first thousand for themselves as salary and picking up whatever they could out of the budget in savings by chiseling on salaries, using stock footage, reverse chases, old sets—and automobile headlights.

The greatest piece of product ever to come out of Poverty Row was John Wayne and although he lingered in its cheap, tawdry, two-bit atmosphere longer than he might have preferred, the Duke was lucky in one respect. He had never been forced to loiter around the drug store or the Gulch bar praying to be picked up for a day's work. Central casting indeed existed, but its services weren't available to Poverty Row, so the cowpokes were grabbed as they showed up.

Not that Duke's early days in pictures as an actor had been without their ups and downs. Or without humiliation. He was really doing pretty well for a young man of the era working on the crew, carpenter, prop man, odd jobs. He got into acting because his physique and his training as a football player led to stunt work. His good looks attracted the attention of two directors, John Ford and Raoul Walsh. Ford gave him bit parts, Raoul sought to make a star out of him in a fabled disaster, *The Big Trail*. That terminated his contract at Fox; another contract with Columbia ended after friction between the young actor and the terrible tempered studio head, Harry Cohn.

Actually, Duke had been around the business for five years before he landed on Poverty Row by way of a contract with Nat Levine, *King of the Quickies*. Like anyone else Duke came to the Row because he needed money.

* * *

The Duke started out in life as Marion Michael Morrison, the first son of Clyde and Mary Morrison on May 27, 1907, in the small town of Winterset, Iowa. Another son, Bob, was born a year or so later.

As a boy, Michael Morrison showed little of the promise that, in a comparatively few years, would make him a star athlete at high school and eventually at college. He was tall, skinny and awkward. He had trouble relating to his fellow students and found it easier to escape from the world around by enjoying the fantasies available to every kid at the movies. He loved Westerns and could empathize with the handsome heroes in white who eventually won over the evil men dressed in black. There were few problems telling the "good guys" from the "bad guys" in silent westerns.

Young Morrison was anything but a replica of his father, "Doc" Morrison, a well built, sturdy, handsome man who had played football, knew the outdoors, and loved to hunt. Afflicted with lung congestion, Clyde Morrison and his family moved to California; first, to Palmdale where his wife fought a losing battle against the perils of the

115

desert, the insects, rattlers, the dust storms and all the other inconveniences her background hadn't prepared her for. So they moved to Glendale, where Clyde, after working for other druggists in the tidy town on the periphery of Los Angeles, and eventually opened his own pharmacy. His sons often helped him at the store.

Clyde was Duke's idol. He passed on to his sons a philosophy of life consisting of three rules: "Always keep your word. A gentleman never insults intentionally. Don't look for trouble, but if you get into a fight make sure you win it." Duke maintains today that he lives by those rules with the exception of the second which he's amended to read: "Never insult anyone unintentionally."

Duke's first ambition was to match his father's hopes for him to become a United States Naval officer, but although he got as far as an "alternate appointment" to Annapolis, it didn't work out. So he went the next best route—getting into college through an athletic scholarship.

In his high school days, Duke had changed from an awkward, stumbling kid into a powerfully built young giant who excelled at all sports. He liked football best. It was rugged, tough, a contact sport—a man to man encounter that fitted his ideal of physical struggle. He won a football scholarship in 1925 at USC, but the largesse available to athletes hadn't grown to the dimensions it has today. Duke could barely get by, but that didn't bother him. He was used to odd jobs, able to find enough to keep him busy—and in funds.

Duke, in his younger days, played handsome sailors opposite pretties like Nan Grey.

A football coach at USC tipped Duke off to the opportunities a husky young man might find at a movie studio. He had connections at Fox, where Tom Mix, Duke's idol, was the reigning star. Mix was a brilliant showman—an actor who never stepped out of character. His tailor-made Western outfits were exclusively white and cream, and he wore them everywhere, to social functions, premieres, parties, to any place where he might be photographed. Mix was making big money and enjoyed living big. He drove long, custom-made cars, convertible so his tanned, smiling face was always visible. His cars were painted white or cream, of course.

Duke not only met Tom Mix but found him friendly and interested in helping him and a pair of other football players the coach had shipped over. The young men were turned over to director George Marshall who put them to work as prop men and set-dressers. The salary came to about thirty-five dollars a week. Having so many football players around, Fox took them for granted. First National didn't. Hollywood was a small world, and when word got around that the studio needed footballers for a Richard Barthelemes picture, *The Drop Kick*, Duke was chosen, and a fleeting frame of film marked his first appearance in 1927.

Duke didn't take it very seriously. He had never thought of acting as a career. He was content with what he was doing. He was making the honor roll at college, earning fairly good money, and helping out his family. Clyde Morrison, evidently ambitious and always on the prowl for money-making ventures, had lost out on another scheme. The Morrisons separated in 1926 and were legally divorced in 1929. Clyde Morrison died several years later after remarrying, and Duke's mother also remarried.

With the break-up in the family, Duke severed his connections with Glendale and was pretty much on his own. He found a surrogate father in John Ford, then and to the day of his death, one of the toughest, most uncompromising directors in the business. Actors maintained he was a sadist, a man who got his kicks from being brutal and insulting to his actors. Still, they longed to work for him because Ford's art was distinctive from the very beginning. Ford liked what he saw in the husky frame and handsome physical appearance Duke presented, and knowing him as a hard worker he began using him in bits.

Much is made in biographies of Duke of how tough Ford was on him, making him do scenes over and over again until they suited his idea of near perfection. That Ford was tough goes without saying, that he'd worry unduly over a bit player seems unlikely. Duke was smart enough to be able to get through his tiny parts with ease. He wasn't a trained actor, but it required nothing special in the way of "method" technique to drive a car—which was more or less the kind of thing Duke generally did.

Ford enjoyed the company of men like himself and Duke became one of the key men in a brawling sort of fraternity that began forming around the director in those silent days—Ward Bond, Bruce Cabot, Victor McLaglen, George O'Brien, Paul Fix and Grant Withers.

Duke got his name, his first taste of fame, his first good role, and a big picture, all at once when Raoul Walsh, acting on Ford's recommendation, cast him in a role Fox hoped to get Gary Cooper for. Cooper was unavailable, so Walsh decided to take a chance on Duke. The film, *The Big Trail*, appeared to have so much else going for it, it didn't really matter who appeared in it.

The Big Trail was the dream of William Fox, a visionary whose visions landed him in jail when his shady deals came to light some years later. But that's another story. *The Big Trail* was to be in wide screen and color. It would dramatize the technical heights the screen was capable of achieving—and did achieve two decades later. But at the time no theatre in America was equipped to handle the special equipment required, and with so much other product available, movie operators weren't about to book it. So *The Big Trail* flopped.

Down the drain went all the hoopla Fox publicists had conjured up about John Wayne. He even went to New York for personal appearances in connection with the image Fox had manufactured for him. They'd written a biography claiming that the Duke was a star football player, an all-American, the dashing romantic who'd dated every girl in Hollywood; they really poured it on. But when the picture flopped, the Duke's contract, which was minimal anyway, was cancelled.

Duke fared no better in his second contract at

Columbia. And there are a lot of tall stories about his problems there. They centered around Harry Cohn, the despotic studio head who ran the plant as his own private empire, brooking no interference. To make sure his serfs were totally in his control, Cohn established an elaborate network of spies—and wasn't beyond spying himself. So the myths have grown and they can be taken for what they're worth. One story has it that they found Duke drunk and sleeping it off one morning on the back lot. Another said that he'd been fooling around with Harry Cohn's private playmate of the moment. Either could be true. It might also have been that maybe, one day, the Duke just didn't show enough deference when he said, "Good morning." Cohn was the kind of executive who would fire a man because he didn't like the color of his necktie.

Cohn's dislike for Wayne became a positive hatred. When option time came, he met the contract clause that raised the young man's salary to three hundred and fifty dollars a week but he spotted him in supporting roles in the two series Columbia was making at the time—westerns starring Buck Jones and Tim McCoy. He also cast him as a crooked football player and loaned him out to Universal for minor parts. This was Cohn's technique of punishment.

But it wasn't all waste. Everywhere John Wayne went he was learning something new. In *The Big Trail* he'd done his own stunts—and Walsh encouraged him. Said Walsh some years later, "He was never the brainiest guy in the business, but he was a kid who kept his word, pretty unusual for an actor. He was always on time, knew what was expected of him and if he didn't know how to do something, he'd ask. That was also pretty unusual."

Working with old pros like Buck Jones and Tim McCoy was an education in itself. Wayne started taking acting seriously. He spent hours in front of a mirror affecting the walk, the squint, the swing of the arms—the tricks of the trade he noticed other actors brought to every performance, accounting for their distinction. He'd always ridden, but now he learned horsemanship as a skill.

In retrospect the tough time Harry Cohn had given him may have been the break of his life— even if it landed him on Poverty Row.

* * *

Early in his career Duke had a reputation as a man who liked his liquor, but everyone who knew him well respected his ability to hold it; those who worked with him understood that his drinking never interfered with his work. He showed up on the set on time, completely prepared for the day's shooting. At the nadir of his depression days, he almost lost a job when he was negotiating to remake some old Ken Maynard Westerns—a tricky, typical Poverty Row device that would combine the long shots of Ken and his men riding the plains and doing their heroics with Wayne working the close-ups and fight scenes. It was all set until the producer balked, telling Duke's agent that he'd heard the actor was a drunk. When the malice got settled it was traced to Harry Cohn; so the producer, not caring much for Cohn, signed Duke and wasn't sorry.

Wayne married his first wife in 1933. She was Josephine Saenz, a dark haired beauty, daughter of the Panamanian consul in Los Angeles. In rapid succession came daughter Toni, son Patrick and a second daughter, Melinda. Supporting a large family in the depression took guts and plenty of hard work. Which is how Wayne got to Nat Levine and started making serials.

Levine was a colorful Hollywood character, short, squat, ugly, with sharp eyes hiding behind thick lenses. He knew more about making movies than any man ever to hit Poverty Row. Any one of them would have made superb production bosses at the bigger plants if they possessed the imagination to understand the greatness of their medium. Virtually all the top assistant directors and production directors of the 50's and 60's were Poverty Row graduates.

Levine was so cheap that even penny-pinchers like the Alexanders loathed him. He went beyond the normal bounds of Poverty Row chiseling. An old-timer like Mr. Stern knew how many telephone calls to make to get his kind of deal. After spending X number of nickels he was ready to compromise. Levine wouldn't. One of Wayne's recollections was working three weeks on a serial for a thousand dollars and starting a second one the following day to save the expense of returning the company from location. Levine worked his company eighteen hours a day, shooting exteriors in the sunlight; interiors at night. Directors like Breezy Eason, who knew their craft, stood still for the pummeling Levine handed them—there was no other place to go.

Levine carried no staff and planned no program for Mascot—even if he announced one grandly at the beginning of each selling year. This wasn't unusual. Even the majors made a big thing out of projecting a huge program of extravaganzas, half of which never reached the writing stage. So between serials, Duke worked where he could—grabbing stunt work if it came along, taking bits in pictures at First National and RKO.

Then along came Monogram, a shade better than most indies because of its management; producer Trem Carr, for example. He was a soft spoken, quiet, dignified man with ambitions for Monogram that he knew could be fulfilled only if the company demonstrated a larger degree of integrity than his confreres along the Gulch. He signed Wayne for a series of Westerns, figuring his name was well enough known, his experience, excellent, his youth, a big advantage. Wayne was younger than the "old men" cowboys who were still holding on. Columbia had turned to young Charles Starrett to carry its Western program, and he and Duke would start a trend away from the old-timers.

Then Herbert Yates entered the scene. He was the owner of Consolidated laboratories, a former Wall Street man, who had acquired the property through speculation and a simple-minded curiosity and interest in the movie business. He wanted to be a producer. Virtually every quickie producer in town was indebted to Consolidated, for the lab had first lien on every foot of film it processed. Yates may not have known much about movie making, but he knew everything about the bank accounts of the sharpies who produced them.

He formed a combine of Mascot, Monogram, a couple of others, and they all headed for the San Fernando Valley where Republic Pictures was started. A United Artists it didn't become. But Yates put money into the plant, built a fine Western street, added some sound stages and, as the producers gradually drifted away back to the States Rights field they understood better, Wayne became about the only property that had been part of the original Republic set-up.

Trem Carr slipped out to form a new Monogram—and life for the next several years was as painful for Duke as it had ever been—if somewhat more rewarding financially. He was steeped in the Western rut and often wondered if he ought to quit. While he headed a group of adventurers called the *Three Mesquiteers*, a series that never seemed to end, Gene Autry came along at Republic and at Paramount the *Hopalong Cassidy* series was created by Harry Sherman who hauled William Boyd out of obscurity to play the dashing, white-haired Hoppy without a line in his handsome face. It was Boyd who prevailed upon Sherman to film the series in color; Boyd who bought the TV rights and Boyd who made a fortune out of the whole *Hopalong* craze, long after he'd been sidelined for the second time in his career. He had simply waited for television instead of fearing it as most Hollywoodites had in the war years when its inevitability was predicted.

Autry was something new—a singing cowboy. He had a cherubic face that would have looked more comfortable behind a grocery counter; as an actor, he was ghastly; as a singer, only slightly better. But Autry had the Midas touch and gold poured into his ten gallon hat as though he had been its inventor. When Autry threatened to bolt Yates' stable, they dug up Roy Rogers, young, handsome, plain, terribly attractive. Roy became an instantaneous hit, so Republic had two big money makers going for it—and the Duke.

Roy must have borrowed one of Autry's hats, for riches began to fill his coffers as, like Autry, he spread his earnings around, investing in real estate, cattle ranches and things cowboys were presumed to know about.

But Duke had his own bag of gold, even if it wasn't opened for him until 1939 when Big Daddy John Ford finally got around to casting him as Ringo Kid in *Stage Coach*, a meaty role that Duke had known existed for a long time. Ford hadn't done a Western in years and was waiting for a propitious time to bring the script out of the trunk.

* * *

Stage Coach was adapted by Dudley Nichols, a top screen writer, from a terse, tight magazine story, *Stage to Lordsburg* by Ernest Haycox, a master of the Western genre. The story brings six desperate characters together on a stage being driven to Lordsburg by a regular driver and a U.S. marshal. They stop to pick up Ringo Kid, an outlaw who has a rendezvous with the Plummer brothers for a showdown. Ringo's horse has gone lame, and the price of the ride is surrender to the marshal. When the coach is attacked by Indians, Ringo becomes vital to the rescue and, after he's settled his score with the Plummers, the marshal looks the other way, allowing Ringo to slip to freedom.

Ford lined up an impressive cast headed by Claire Trevor, Thomas Mitchell, John Carradine, George Bancroft and Andy Devine. He chose Monument Valley as the location and battled to cast Wayne as Ringo. The next step involved Wayne's persuading Herbert Yates to consent to the loanout. It took effort but eventually Wayne made his first giant step toward super-stardom. No one ever imagined—perhaps John Ford saw it— how far Duke would travel after *Stage Coach*.

Tiresome Walter Wanger didn't, for he was the producer who had to be convinced that a B picture actor was up to the part—much less worthy of being in a Wanger picture. Afterward, Wanger took credit for discovering Wayne, but that was to be expected. He also maintained that buying the Haycox story was his idea. Ford, however, kept Wanger at a safe distance. When the producer visited the location he was horrified to find Duke doing his own stunts—a situation the actor and Ford took for granted.

One of Wayne's biographers, Maurice Zolotow, a skilled reporter, wrote that a souvenir program distributed at the Westwood theatre press preview of *Stage Coach* contained such extravagant praise of Wanger's role in the production that a separate page had to be slipped inside it to acknowledge that such talents as Ford, Dudley Nichols and Ernest Haycox indeed existed. I was at the Westwood screening and can't recall the program, but that's a problem of memory. It was just the sort of thing Wanger was given to.

Zolotow suggests that Wayne was disappointed by the equivocal notices *Stage Coach* and his own performance received from the *New York Times* and *Herald-Tribune*—as though equivocation were suddenly new to those papers. In its arts section (except for Ada Louise's Huxtable's reports on architecture), *Times* critics still hem and haw—except that today their commentary has grown longer, aimed largely at movie buffs who idolize obscure directors like Samuel Fuller and have memorized all the dialogue from *The Wizard of Oz*.

Yet, when Wayne faced the critics in *Red River* several years later, Bosley Crowther was hardly playing mumbledy-peg when he wrote in the *Times* that the many excellent performances were "topped off by a withering job of acting a boss-wrangler done by Mr. Wayne. This consistently able portrayer of two-fisted, two-gunned outdoor men surpasses himself in this picture."

The main event of that night at the Westwood Village theatre seems to have been overlooked by the historians—as well as the major protagonist—

"Stage Coach" raised John Wayne to stardom. He and Claire Trevor headed an all-star cast.

John Wayne. From the minute Duke appeared on the screen and steadily brought the Ringo Kid into focus there was absolutely no doubt that the audience was witnessing the birth of an important new star, a big man in the same big league as Gary Cooper. If there were any references to his oateater background, they resolved themselves into wondering, "How is the poor sonuvabitch going to get out of Republic?"

Praise for the picture was universally enthusiastic; for a change Wanger didn't have to bribe reviewers. And Duke Wayne became the talk of the industry. For obvious reasons. He was the surprise. *Stage Coach* was a class Western, handsomely mounted, with an action-filled, suspenseful story, fascinating characters, a John Ford masterpiece. And what could one write that hadn't already been printed about Thomas Mitchell, Claire Trevor, Carradine and Donald Meek? Inevitably, Wayne grabbed all the space.

Another biographer, Alan G. Barbour, begins his pictorial and thorough examination of Wayne's professional work with: "Most critics do not particularly care for John Wayne. They dislike his films, heap scorn on his performances, are appalled by his politics and, indeed, find no real interest in the man himself."

That's covering a lot of territory and is hardly substantiated by the pile of clippings accumulated for this comparatively short piece on Wayne—clippings of reviews and feature stories which I found fascinating because of the warmth of the articles—especially from writers who candidly admitted being "appalled by his politics."

Humphrey Bogart used to take a dim view of actors belonging to the "Aw shucks, gee whiz, I'm not an actor," school. Bogie fumed, "It seems to me that if they don't consider themselves actors, then they must be in the wrong business."

John Wayne has never been guilty of that brand of thinking. He's well aware of who he is and what he represents as an actor, "When I came in," he claims, "the western man never lost his white hat and always rode the white horse and waited for the man to get up again in the fight. If a guy hit me with a vase, I'd hit him with a chair. That's the way we played it. I also paid attention to the girl, kissed her if I felt it suited the situation. I changed the saintly Boy Scout of the original cowboy into a more normal kind of fella."

But his personal image was hardly improved when, in talking about his nomination for the Oscar he eventually won for *True Grit*, Duke told Chicago newsman Roger Ebert, "I was nominated for *Sands of Iwo Jima*, but I didn't win. Maybe this time they'll review the picture instead of me. That little clique back there in the East has taken great personal satisfaction in reviewing my politics instead of my pictures."

You expect petulance from disgruntled youngsters who think they're being abused but not from an old pro who knows differently. Obviously, when the nomination came to him he could expect enthusiasm from old friends around town like

Maureen O'Hara, John Ford, Jimmy Stewart and Andrew McLaglen. But even such an anti-establishmentarian as Steve McQueen is a Wayne fan. "Sometimes kids ask me what a pro is," he said, "I just point to the Duke."

Terry Robbins, a Chicago coordinator for the radical S.D.S. at the time he was asked about Wayne said, "I consider Wayne terrific and total. He's tough, down to earth, and he says and acts what he believes. He's completely straight and really groovy. If they wanted to really make a movie about Che Guevara, they ought to have Wayne play him." Abbie Hoffman volunteered, "I like Wayne's wholesomeness, his style. As for his politics, well..."

One mild review by two snob newspapers of *Stage Coach* does not compose an actor's scrap book. The fact is that whenever Zolotow and Barbour needed reviews to substantiate appreciation for Wayne, they found the best commentary in the pages of the Eastern clique, the *New York Times* where today's Vincent Canby has been as fulsome in his praise as Bosley Crowther ever was, and Andrew Sarris of *The Village Voice* whose commentary has never confused Wayne's politics with his art.

But Duke's carried the chip on his shoulder so long it won't fall off, as he continued to beef in the Ebert interview.

"It seems nobody remembers how different the fellows were in *The Quiet Man* or *Iwo Jima* or *Yellow Ribbon*, when I was thirty-five playing a man sixty-five. To stay a star, you have to bring along some of your personality. Thousands of good actors can carry a scene, but a star has to carry the scene and still, without intruding, allow some of his character into it."

Here Duke makes sense instead of parroting his friend, Spiro Agnew, who certainly didn't enrich his short and shabby political career with his remarks about the Eastern Establishment. It remains very much in business, sturdily surviving the barbs of public figures who mistakenly assume that divisiveness is the key to Middle America. They insult Middle America's sense of proportion. Duke Wayne could never have run the thousands of cattle along the range of a hundred odd Westerns if the Eastern Establishment weren't there to buy them. No man who has been before the public for nearly fifty years, thirty-five as a major star, has much to complain about. He's been paid handsomely, if that counts at this stage of his life; he has been honored by his peers, adored by millions of fans and accorded the respect his talents deserve. Becoming a querulous old man, sniveling about Establishment newspapers, ill suits the tall-in-the-saddle image Wayne has spent a lifetime creating. But pettiness has been an old Wayne character defect. As friends grudgingly admit, "Duke can be awfully small time."

Seen objectively, Wayne's career is a triumph of artistry and durability, layered with the special magnetism (and in his younger days, sex appeal) that sets a super-star apart. There wasn't a handsomer, taller, sexier looking man around than Duke in his thirties when *Stage Coach* lifted him from obscurity. It took him a long time to outgrow romantic leads. When he decided to age, he did it beautifully as *True. Grit* demonstrated. The New York papers found his romp with Katharine Hepburn in *Rooster Cogburn*, the kind of battle between two old pros that makes movies the fun they should be.

Of course Wayne uses tricks. Every actor does and they go about creating them with all the skill at their command. The use of tricks is the secret of their effectiveness. Wayne is a master magician in this area. He knows how to roll full steam ahead, when to simmer down, exactly the second to pull back from that one big bite of the scenery when he compels the audience to feel rather than see. Wayne, when the words and the action are there to work with, is a craftsman who'll be studied long after his whining about the "Wayne thing" has been forgotten.

A man who's been around as long as Wayne couldn't avoid a bomb now and then, and Wayne, with his total recall, takes amused pride both in the clinkers and his own checkered career. Better for the moviegoer to recall his private highlights and cherish them—*Stage Coach, Iwo Jima, Pittsburgh* (I'm a minority there), *Wake of the Red Witch, The Shepherd of the Hills, The Quiet Man* and *Fort Apache*. And, of course, *The Long Voyage Home*. Eugene O'Neill might have had Wayne in mind when he wrote the sea stories which John Ford used as the basis for this jewel of a movie. No one slurred Wayne's work in that picture—so totally different from anything he'd been identified with before, down to the difficult Swedish accent which Wayne mastered.

I'm pretty sure that my list of Wayne favorites was born of the entertainment they offered—not from sitting in a theatre and thinking, "Gosh, I'm seeing a real patriot." Or the qualities youthful authorities on old movies tend to explain as Wayne's "built-in mysticism", his association with those old and revered qualities of courage, honor, respect for the flag, the law, women and motherhood. I shouldn't be the least surprised that Cher possesses these very same qualities, but isn't it her navel audiences generally notice?

* * *

After *Stage Coach*, there was some hard negotiating to be done with Republic and by this time Duke and his agents carried clout. They couldn't stop Republic from reissuing the *Three Mesquiteers* series to capitalize on Duke's step out of B's and cheap horse operas. But concessions were made on all sides and Wayne finished his obligations to the Valley independent. His next outside picture was at RKO, *Allegheny Uprising*, and for the first time in his life Duke knew the feelings of being a star. There was no let-up in the demand for his services as he moved from studio to studio, impressing top directors and producers with his professionalism. And, at the same time, building up a vast public that gave potency to his name on a marquee.

The average star, given Duke's break in *Stage*

Coach and the opportunities that came afterward, would have rushed through the Republic contract (even to working on weekends) and gotten away from the connotations of the name. For all its hopes and dreams, Republic was never cut out to become a major in the sense understood in the movie business at the time—another MGM, 20th Century or Paramount. Yates was not the man for the job and he didn't have talent in large enough bundles. Republic eventually lost Autry and Rogers—and it would part company with Wayne even if Duke and Yates sat down in 1946 to write a new and what was considered a very favorable contract for the star. It was a deal which made him the first actor-producer since Charles Chaplin, the head of his own unit at Republic, yet free to accept assignments at any other studio he chose.

But 1946 wasn't the year for the best-intentioned movie men to work out partnerships tying them up for several years. Especially for capitalists. Old Hollywood and its world-wide monopoly on theatres, studios, talent, distribution, was under attack from all sides. The government had cut it down to size with a series of anti-trust suits that broke up the marriages of the studios and theatres and ended the block booking of pictures. Exhibitors instead bid for individual movies—a privilege they fought for thirty years ago and regret bitterly today.

There was the threat of television, and Hollywood buried its head in the sand at the mention of the medium. Executives were shocked by the neorealism of films like *Bicycle Thief* which came out of Italy before the dust of war had barely settled over Europe. "A kid pissing on the streets? My God!" They paid little attention to the fact that first, the Italian government; then France and England saw movies as a quick route to needed American dollars, so government subsidies turned film production in those countries from speculative enterprises to government-insured exports.

At home, postwar movie attendance was beginning to drop. The reasons lay beyond television and the dribble of European imports. Filmgoers had had their fill of the Hollywood style—the glossy musical, the formula Western, the *Jones Family, Blondie*, American musicals about Coney Island and Atlantic City.

Hollywood's postwar product barely survived because movie going was still the national habit. That gradually changed when gasoline became plentiful, as new cars came off the assembly lines, bowling alleys opened up and other forms of entertainment drew on the strength of the movie dollar. Within four short years, some of the top talent in Hollywood would be working in Europe, representing a cross-section of the old movie colony. They included Frank Sinatra, Cary Grant, Humphrey Bogart, John Ireland, David Niven, Dennis O'Keefe, Robert Taylor, Kirk Douglas, Mario Lanza; actresses Ava Gardner, Audrey Hepburn, Deborah Kerr, Katharine Hepburn, Jennifer Jones, Linda Christian, Claudette Colbert; producers and directors Gregory Ratoff, Joseph Mankiewicz, Anatole Litvak, Robert Rossen, Henry Mathaway, Michael Curtiz, Henry Koster, Stanley Kramer, Alfred Hitchcock; writers Irwin Shaw, Edward Anhalt, and virtually all the blacklisted survivors of the Hollywood Witch Hunt. The Via Venta was nicknamed "The Beach," and they called Rome "Hollywood on the Tiber."

When the mighty Darryl Zanuck, production head of 20th Century-Fox, abandoned his studio job to head his own unit in Paris, there were harsh words between him and the Duke over what Hollywood called "runaway production." Eventually Duke went to Ireland for *The Quiet Man*, to Libya for *Legend of the Lost* and seriously considered Peru for *The Alamo*.

* * *

With fame there came change and a young man who one day was simply hustling bread for his wife and kids gradually became a complicated individual caught up in a super-active life that divided itself into three distinct and demanding parts: his professional world as an actor-producer, his private life and Duke's curious role as a political spokesman for Hollywood's conservative wing, referred to move commonly by its opponents—and victims—as reactionary.

That Duke chose conservatism as his political philosophy was not curious; that this genial, easygoing graduate of Poverty Row, who enjoyed a rowdy night out on the town with his buddies, who was worshipped by his family and friends as "the finest" would take on the headaches of politicking seemed totally out of character.

Anything but curious was the old truth that when a man spreads himself so thin, something is bound to break, and the first wound is inflicted on his marriage.

In many respects, the Wayne marriage had been a happy one—the fulfillment of the family both partners wanted—the birth of the children, Michael, Melinda and Patrick. There had been the sharing of hard times when Duke was a thousand dollar a picture serial star for Nat Levine, rising at four, getting home at midnight, spending weeks on location, jumping from one picture to another overnight.

Josephine had been brought up differently. She was a genteel young woman, well educated, who preferred a social life comparable to what she presumed she was, a star's wife. She did move personally in a gracious society within the world of women like Loretta Young. Josie was uncomfortable with Duke's companions—those hard-drinking pals like Grant Withers and Ward Bond who seemed to live their tough guy roles off screen.

Duke admitted that after about four years theirs had become a marriage in name only. For all the bravado of his extroverted personality Duke chose to keep his private life private. There was a separation in 1942 and a divorce a couple of years later which Josie filed with the explanation that it was strictly a legal action as far as she was concerned since her religion forbade divorce.

Duke's only comment, made privately to

friends, said, "Josie spent so much time being a lady that she forgot how to be a woman."

The separation years kept the gossip columnists busy. Duke was linked romantically with a succession of women—most happened to be the leading ladies of his movies, the majority, foreign. Marlene Dietrich became a name that figured prominently in the gossip column accounts of Duke's romantic capers—along with Paulette Goddard, Sigrid Gurie and Osa Massen. Only Miss Massen never appeared opposite him; they became friends when he sought her out to help him with the Swedish accent required for *Long Voyage Home*.

For all the grimness of his political pronouncements Duke is not without a sense of humor. And those "establishment writers" who come prepared to meet an ogre invariably go away charmed by Duke's unfailing good manners, quiet politeness, the twinkle in his eye and relish of the jokes he tells on himself.

Duke has never spoken publicly about Vera Hruba Ralston, a young, blonde Czechoslovakian ice skater with whom Herbert Yates, aged sixty-one, had fallen in love. Deeply enough to want to make her a star. And what better route than casting her opposite Duke? He endured the experience in *Dakota* and *The Fighting Kentuckian*. Yates' childish jealousy kept Duke and Vera under constant surveilance by the producer's network of spics, and the couple of visits Duke made to the lady's dressing room for rehearsal and to help Vera with her English drove Yates wild.

**Wayne's third wife, Pilar, and daughter Aissa.
They live apart now but remain in touch daily.**

Duke only chuckles when Vera's name comes up these days. What Yates didn't want to believe was that Vera Hruba was the industry laughing stock and for Duke to even consider muscling in would have made him appear as foolish as his partner. But a little teasing of the old boy was permissible. Republic stockholders eventually revolted against the fortune lavished on non-star Vera and the ice skater settled for marriage, eventually becoming a very rich widow. One of the more unbelievable spectacles of Hollywood night life during the Yates-Vera Hruba courtship was the sight of the old man on the dance floors of Mocambo and Ciro's whirling his lady around with razzamatazz that Gene Kelly could envy.

During the final faltering years of his marriage Duke often visited Mexico. On one of these trips he met a pretty young Mexican actress named Esperanza Diaz Ceballow Bauer whose nickname was "Chata"—"pugnose" in English. Theirs was stormy courtship and a stormy marriage when it started in January 1946 and ended in bitterness in 1953 when Esperanza, with noted criminal lawyer Jerry Giesler as her attorney went into court with a series of charges against Wayne that described him as an inhuman monster. She complained of beatings, infidelity, drunkenness and on the stand seemed to relish recalling the intimate details of her life with Wayne. Wayne had successfully avoided scandal in his career and it smarted. Taking the stand in his own defense he denied the charges categorically and women outside the court carried signs saying, "Duke, you can clobber me any time."

Esperanza was granted a settlement of fifty thousand dollars a year for six years. She returned to Mexico—a shattered woman, victim of alcoholism, her unfulfilled ambition to become an actress, perhaps even disappointed at having failed at being a good wife to a man who had lavished on her things she never dreamed existed—beautiful homes, exciting trips, everything his money could buy. In his face she flaunted her own unfaithfulness and the marriage deteriorated into one sullen day after the other, the atmosphere charged with hatred, alternating with moments of ecstasy. About a year after her return to Mexico, Esperanza had dissipated her annuity, moved into squalid quarters, turned her back on the world, drank tequila day after day. In the fall she was found in her dingy rooms—dead of a heart attack.

It was a sordid experience in Duke's life, and friends eventually pieced together the story of a man insanely in love with a woman who was enslaved by alcohol and dominated by an alcoholic mother who believed in corporal punishment and inflicted the beatings Duke was accused of. Duke's illusions about Chata's character were shattered one by one. He hoped to find in her a wife who would understand the nature of his work and forgive the irregularity of his hours, a woman who would try to make a home under conditions which would never be ideal. Esperanza simply lacked the capacity to understand what was expected. She resented sacrificing her own ambitions which would have come to nothing under any circumstances. Duke, surrounded by drunks, had made the fatal mistake of marrying one.

Then there came Pilar Palette, a beauty he met in Peru while he was scouting locations for his production, *The Alamo*.

* * *

In the years of his final separation from Josie and the desperate months of his tragic relationship with Esperanza, Duke made about twenty major pictures—plus a few B's remaining on his Republic contract. Pearl Harbor occurred in 1941, and Duke tried to enlist but met rejection because of his family status and age.

Like a number of actors who couldn't perform, Duke bravely put together some sort of routine and was a hit wherever he went, just by talking to the men in the war zones, carrying messages from home and giving them encouragement. He had become one of the most popular stars in films, and his name became a regular at the top of the "ten best box office stars" in an annual poll of thousands of exhibitors across the country. Gary Cooper and Duke played see-saw over the years, switching back and forth from first to second as though the top of the poll belonged exclusively to them.

The extent of Wayne's exposure was one explanation of his popularity. As Duke became a bigger star, reissues of his old movies often played at the same time with the new pictures of this period that included the Howard Hawks' production of *Red River, Reap the Wild Wind* which brought him into the majestic orbit of Cecil B. DeMille, and *She Wore a Yellow Ribbon*, which John Ford directed and which started a friendship between Duke and Howard Hughes.

After some preliminary pre-signing bouts, Duke got along fine with the mighty DeMille, who had promised the feisty actor that there'd be no humiliating him in public. He kept his word and Duke regretted not having worked again with DeMille. Hughes, always unpredictable, was like "the man who came to dinner," given to dropping in on his star at odd hours of the day or night. Duke took the surprise visits with good humor; any diversion was welcome to arouse him from the deep depression of his marriage—depression and anxieties magnified by Duke's guilt, fear that he was responsible, inability to see the end of a messy, insufferable way of life.

No wonder that he plunged into work with such grim determination, holding on to the long hours at the studio and on location as precious moments when his mind was free of any thought but the immediate task—the need for living in the "now"—not forecasting the horrors of the future.

Then, in 1944, there came the organization of the Motion Picture Alliance for the Preservation of American Ideals. Its first public meeting was held at the Beverly Wilshire Hotel, attended by about fifteen hundred persons, representing all the craft unions in the industry and a group of top stars that included Gary Cooper, Irene Dunne, Barbara Stanwyck, Ginger Rogers, Ward Bond, Clark Gable, Robert Montgomery and Adolphe Menjou. Other notables were musical director Dimitri Tiomkin, producers William Goetz, Cecil B. De-Mille, Mike Frankovitch; directors Norman Taurog, Sam Wood, Victor Fleming, John Ford. The lone studio head present was Walt Disney. Labor was represented by Roy Brewer.

A far less impressive group of screen writers was composed of Frank Gruber, Borden Chase, James Edward Grant, James Kevin McGuinness (who also produced), Richard English, Howard Emmett Rogers, John McCauley and Morris Ryskind.

Of the lot, Ryskind was the most distinguished, having won the Pulitzer Prize, for *Of Thee I Sing* the first musical play to achieve the honor. Ryskind also wrote numerous Marx Brothers pictures. Ryskind admirers didn't feel he quite belonged in such a group—but there he was.

The writers, however, were the powers behind the formation of the Alliance, the fellows who wrote the speeches, made the policy and did the thinking for the others. They were the right wingers who had suffered a crushing defeat in the organization of the Screen Writers Guild and its ultimate recognition as an instrument for collective bargaining with the studios. They had lost out in writing the Guild's constitution and in fielding their slate of officers—defeated by a militant, vocal, labor-minded group of liberals. The alliance was evidently their answer to the new union.

146

The first question reporters should have asked was, "Who paid the rent for the Beverly Wilshire grand ballroom that night?" and much more would have been understood about the Alliance. There were other questions. Why was Roy Brewer present? Was he acting as an individual, an undercover man for the producers or as the top labor executive in Hollywood, an observer on behalf of his constituency? Adolphe Menjou's presence was obvious. The once excellent actor, noted for his sophisticated roles and fabled wardrobe, had become fanatical on the subject of Communism and had been making lists of subversives for years, listing suspect barbers and waiters at posh restaurants whose accents were suspicious. The Alliance could use Menjou either as house goat or effective speaker.

Sam Wood, Norman Taurog and Victor Fleming enjoyed close ties with Metro-Goldwyn-Mayer, Wood and Fleming being under contract. So were Robert Taylor, always willing to show up where the studio wanted him and Robert Montgomery, very much his own man. But Montgomery had changed over the years since he led the actors in the fight for the Guild and became its first president.

With so much MGM present, the Alliance origins would have to tunnel back to Louis B. Mayer, the "great tycoon" who cherished political string pulling as much as persuading stars like Jeanette MacDonald and Miliza Korjus to sit on his lap while they signed their contracts. Mayer, it was said, had a direct line to the White House when Herbert Hoover was president and whoever sat in the Governor's chair at Sacramento maintained a connection with L.B. His was a bottomless purse, implemented by his control of a stable of stars, brainwashed to participate in his reactionary Republican politics.

Director Sam Wood was elected president of the Alliance and it was agreed that regular meetings would be held thereafter at the American Legion auditorium in Hollywood. At first, the Alliance caused little stir in Hollywood, having been formed at a time when groups proliferated in such numbers that it had become virtually impossible to keep track of them.

Political activists were not new to show business, and when you dug up their roots they led to the labor struggle. Producers battled unionization; they paid tribute to Al Capone's goons as the price of labor peace and rigged elections to get company stooges into office of independent unions like the Screen Actors Guild.

It was an old and sad story whose sordidness could be traced back to the Actors' Strike of 1919 when George M. Cohan sided with the producers against his brother actors, creating an atmosphere of suspicion within theatrical unions that persists to this day.

The genesis of the Alliance was the liberal victory in the Screen Writers Guild. That had been the last straw and it was interpreted by the losers as symptomatic of a *malaise* embracing all the professional guilds. They feared that a small group of Communists, under party discipline, would take over the unions and control American movies. The first meetings were held at the home of James Kevin McGuinness, an MGM writer and producer. Wayne attended one of these informal discussions, brought by old friend, Ward Bond. He said nothing but listened as McGuinness, Sam Wood and others discussed the Communist dangers existing in Hollywood. Wayne said nothing but was concerned by the writers' warning of a "commie takeover of the Screen Writers Guild."

In 1969, Duke told *Time Magazine*: "There's a lot of yella bastards in this country who would like to call patriotism 'old-fashioned.' With all that leftist activity I was quite obviously on the other side. I was invited to a couple cell meetings, and I played the lamb to listen to 'em for a while. The only guy that ever fooled me was the director Edward Dmytryk. I made a picture with him called *Back to Bataan*. He started talking about the masses, and as soon as he started using that word—which is from their book—not ours—I knew he was a Commie."

(Dmytryk, called before the House Un-American Activities, at first took the Fifth Amendment but admitted later that he had been a Communist between 1944 and 1945 and had undergone a change of heart.)

Continued *Time*: Senator Joseph McCarthy and the House Un-American Committee were uncovering more leftists back East, the Hollywood Ten were cited for contempt, and Wayne decided that it was time to help out. "An actor is part of a bigger world than Hollywood," he announced. Together with Scenarist Chase and such rigid stalwarts as

Actors Adolphe Menjou and Ward Bond, Wayne helped to form the Motion Picture Alliance for the Preservation of American Ideals. Wayne may have seen himself as a patriot. But next to some of his red-white-and-blue-blooded colleagues he looked a little pink. "We had a split in the group," Chase later reported, "the once-a-Communist-always-a-Communist group and the group that thought it was ridiculous to destroy some of those who, say joined the party in the '30s in Nazi Germany. Duke and I were in the latter group." A risky place to be; when Wayne praised Larry Parks for admitting his Old Left indiscretions, Hedda Hopper bawled out the Duke publicly. He got the message. "I think those blacklisted people should have been sent over to Russia," he now declares. "They'd have been taken care of over there, and if the Commies ever won over here, why hell, those guys would be the first ones they'd take care of—after me." Still, even when he became president of the Alliance, Wayne viewed politics as a necessary evil. "My main object in making a motion picture is entertainment," he confesses. "If at the same time I can strike a blow for liberty, then I'll stick one in."

The Alliance and the House Un-American Activities Committee cast twin specters of fear over Hollywood. On his side of the fence, Duke claims that anyone affiliated with the Alliance was branded an anti-Semite, a Nazi and, in his case, a lout, drunk, clown and faithless husband. It was maintained that until the Alliance came into existence, known conservatives like Adolphe

Menjou had suffered blacklisting, along with writers like Jim McGuinness. Pat O'Brien blamed his affiliation for difficulty in finding roles as a free-lance actor.

Lists begat lists and besides those compiled by the Un-American Activities, there was one figured out by the Alliance and another subversive list in Sacramento compiled by State Senator Kenny. The Kenny list was as thick as the telephone book—it used symbols to designate how subversive an individual was. Among the names were Darryl Zanuck's and mine with a designation that could have been SOB. When you looked up SOB in the appendix it revealed that Zanuck and I had both read papers at a Writers' Congress held on the campus of the University of Southern California.

Clark Gable succeeded Sam Wood as president of the Alliance to be followed by Robert Taylor and finally, in 1948, Wayne became president. According to Maurice Zolotow, Wayne supported a resolution by Roy Brewer that "Los Angeles, with the second largest representation of Communists in America, should register all Communists."

There were the absurdities, yes, that made the Alliance ridiculous. And there were the laughs in Washington when the Un-American Committee asked Lionel Stander if he had ever attended Communist Cell meetings, "Sure," he said. Asked why, the gravel-voiced comedian answered, "To meet girls."

Others could not be so flip. Some went to jail for contempt of Congress—for refusing to identify themselves as Communists, a legal political party in all forty-eight states. The point of confrontation between the Congressional Committee and those summoned for hearings was the right of the individual to keep his political affiliations private, personal, and secret. For the witnesses to have identified themselves as Communists, assuming some were, exposed them to naming others. Or incriminating themselves if Congress suddenly decided that, like the Japanese-Americans, Communists represented a danger and threat to the country's security. It was tricky debating, hence the lawyers for the Hollywood victims chose the Fifth Amendment as the logical route of defense. This invited a charge of contempt of Congress and possible prison, a penalty not generally associated with political activity in the United States.

Yet Chairman Martin Dies brandished his whips and talented men were jailed: Dalton Trumbo, Ring Lardner, Jr., Adrian Scott, John Howard Lawson, all brilliant writers, producers and directors. Dymytryk was among them but, as has been noted, he recanted. Lardner and Scott ultimately died; their friends blaming the experience for their deteriorating health. Then there were those who were simply labelled "unfriendly witnesses" when they refused to answer the so-called $64 Question, "Are you now or have you ever been a member of the Communist Party?" They automatically suffered the blacklist; brilliant careers snuffed out overnight; among them, Academy Award winner Gale Sondergaard, Anne Revere, J. Edward Bromberg, Will Geer, Larry Parks—so many others.

They gave Duke Wayne an Oscar for his triumph as feisty Rooster Cogburn in "True Grit."

The Committee called Judy Holliday and Arthur Miller—even Lucille Ball. But nothing much happened to them because they appeared bewildered by it all and there were friends in high places.

There were also suicides. Philip Loeb, a beautiful Broadway actor, who had been playing in *The Goldbergs* for years on radio.

There was the tragedy of John Garfield—he was on all the lists, but the Dies boys never subpoenaed him. Finally, long after the hue and cry had died down, he appeared as a "voluntary, friendly witness" and proclaimed his patriotism, insisting he had never been a Party member. It was a lonely decision—and it came too late. His career had already been wrecked; alcoholism did the rest. Garfield died prematurely at thirty-nine of a heart attack. Carl Foreman, the author and co-producer of *High Noon*, fled to Europe, so did Sidney Buchman, a distinguished intellectual, who had produced the two *Al Jolson* pictures.

The cruelty of the Alliance, the self-serving publicity the Un-American Committee generated for itself—these obvious tricks were not appreciated by the public-at-large. Older filmgoers, remembering the Great Depression, could understand how young actors had been lured into Communist membership. Although the American Legion heads constantly threatened "picket" and "boycott" of movies employing "Commie Rats" there was no groundswell of support from rank and file members. The Witch Hunt produced no uproar for the heads of the personalities named as Reds. The public didn't give a damn. The Alliance was recognized for what it was—an illegal vigilante group.

And, alas, the blacklist was as old in America as Show Biz itself. Back in the vaudeville days, crusty old E.F. Albee barred *Variety* from his office because it supported the efforts of vaudevillians to organize. He banned Eva Tanguay from the theatres he controlled, banished Nora Bayes or anyone else who crossed his path. Alexander Pantages controlled the prized Pantages time on the Coast and pretty young things who didn't accept invitations to his private office weren't surprised when their acts were cancelled.

Attitudes have softened since the fifties when the Alliance changed the rules for blackballing from sex to politics. And Zolotow reports a significant switch by Duke Wayne when, after reading the screenplay of *True Grit* and accepting the lead, he got a telephone call saying that the author, Marguerite Roberts, had attended meetings of the Communist Party faction in the Screen Writers' Guild twenty years previously.

"Wayne blew his stack," wrote Zolotow. "He told the informant, in a blaze of profanity, that he did not care what Miss Roberts had done years before, but that the script was a fine script, and it expressed American principles, and he did not give a damn what a person had once been or once done."

Duke could modify his attitudes when his own interests were affected. Carlo Ponti's agreement with Wayne's Batjac productions in lending

Sophia Loren for *Legend of the Lost* stipulated that the company would pay the salary and expenses of an able secretary-manager who had accompanied her before. An amiable, friendly, talented man, he was also a Communist in good standing in Italy. Wayne puzzled over this for days until a compromise was reached. The man's name wouldn't appear on the Batjac payroll but on that of United Artists, the picture's distributor!

* * *

Eventually the Alliance was shamed out of existence, and the Un-American Committee, after years of idleness, was quietly retired. What had all the hysteria of those years, the accusations, the counter-accusations produced? No bombs were found in the garages of the men who went to prison nor in the apartments of the ladies who were drummed out of Hollywood. No subversive movies were made although, according to Robert Taylor in his Congressional testimony, MGM did a naughty when at the request of the *State Department*, it made a boxoffice bomb, *The Song of Russia*.

But interest in the era of the Red Witch Hunt has awakened the curiosity of historians who have begun to sift the records with care. They have discovered that innuendo was preferred to facts, flag-waving substituted for documentation, that little kids were barred from working in the movies and on TV because their mothers and fathers had attended rallies of organizations sponsored by Governor and Mrs. Herbert Lehman, Eleanor

Roosevelt and the Honorable Fiorello LaGuardia, mayor of the City of New York.

The Alliance had its East Coast counterpart—*Red Channels*—an organization which paid informants five dollars a head for the names of suspected Communists and let it be known that names could be removed from the blacklist for a fee—paid directly to Red Channels' officials or by making a "confession" to a prominent newspaper columnist, George Sokolsky.

Last year an excellent TV production *Trial by Fear* recorded the trials of commentator John Henry Falk who fought the blacklist with the help of attorney Louis Nizer. Lillian Hellman, the distinguished playwright, has written about and begun to speak publicly of those dark years when her work was banned in Hollywood.

Dalton Trumbo, still a liberal, ever a pragmatist, wins Awards today for screenplays written under his own name instead of the pseudonym Richard Rich, the name by which he won an Award in the fifties. There was dead silence at the Academy ceremonies when no Mr. Rich appeared to claim the prize.

Of the early members of the Alliance, some have gone on to that great Beverly Wilshire ballroom in the sky; others are seldom heard from—certainly not in the context of their work with the Alliance. All but Duke (he doesn't dwell on those days) who is still active enough politically to have been at the end of a rumor in 1972 that he had been selected as George Wallace's running mate for the presidency. Duke answered "bullshit" and the papers, taking him at his word, printed DUKE SAYS B——————T TO WALLACE RUMORS.

As a matter of fact, Duke talks on and on. The following represent some samples, culled at random:

To magazine writer Guy Flatley, at the depth of the Watergate scandal he said, "They're trying to crucify Richard Nixon, but when they're writing the Watergate history of this period, Watergate will be no more than a footnote. Believe me, I have high respect for the bulldogged way in which our President has been able to administrate this government, in spite of the articulate liberal press—whose only purpose is to sell toilet paper and Toyotas—and in spite of ambitious politicians who would deny him the help and encouragement a man needs to face the problems of this country."

To the same writer, Duke weighed these words in respect to a query about Spiro Agnew, "I endorsed Spiro Agnew's attitudes, but I knew nothing of his private affairs. I was sadly disappointed to discover he had feet of clay."

To Robert Lardine he said, "The Reds are working on the kids. The Communists said it very plainly that the working man is a difficult person to swing over if he's making a living wage. So they're concentrated on the youngsters.

"Teachers are really a problem. More of them are radical than the students. Many kids in school oppose the radical view, but they're afraid to express their opinions because the teachers may take it out on them by lowering their grades."

The Communists are also at fault for the racial

crisis, Wayne said, "They're definitely helping to promote trouble with the blacks. I think the blacks shouldn't overreact. I went without a few meals plenty of times, and I don't feel that Rockefeller and the church owe me lots of money."

Current Biography concluded its account of Wayne's career with this paragraph: "The actor has been a conspicuous political reactionary, a fervent anti-Communist, and an unabashed patriotic chauvinist, since he helped to found the Motion Picture Alliance for the Preservation of American Ideals in 1944. A Republican, he has campaigned for Barry Goldwater, Ronald Reagan, and Richard Nixon, and he spoke at the 1968 Republican National Convention in Miami, Florida. About civil rights, he has said: 'I believe in white supremacy until the blacks are educated to a point of responsibility. I don't believe in giving authority and positions of leadership to irresponsible people.' Having conservative tastes in general, he deplores the lattitude given sex and violence in motion pictures (He insists that his straight-shooting, two-fisted screen violence had been different, sort of tongue-in-cheek.)"

* * *

Pilar Palette was a young Peruvian actress, just twenty-seven when she married Duke in 1954, who was nineteen years older. She was a well-established film star when Duke visited Lima a year or so earlier. She wasn't especially bowled over by meeting the world's *Numero Uno* boxoffice

159

star. But when they met again—Pilar had come to Hollywood to finish up some work on a picture—it was a different story. She liked the rugged, handsome, blue-eyed actor and after a whirlwind courtship they settled down together and married on November 1, 1954, a marriage that produced three children, Aissa, John Ethan and Marisa.

Pilar was quite a change from Duke's previous wives, a cool young woman who, having been a professional, took the Wayne life style for what it was. There were no hopes for changing it, and why? She got along well with Duke's friends; she enjoyed location, and the Wayne buddies basked in the warmth of her charm and genuine affection for them. It was remarkable how well she fitted into things.

Not that there weren't rough storms now and then—life with Duke has turbulence written into it—but for once Duke found a woman whose strength matched his, a woman capable of being just as blunt, direct and honest. So instead of quarrels becoming the end of the world, they became reasons for making up and renewing an affection that appeared to deepen with the years. The luckiest break of Duke's life was having Pilar at his side when he was hit with the Big C—and if you want to include a professional note, to enjoy the comfort of his quiet moments with her when he was being slaughtered for The *Green Berets* and *The Alamo*.

The Alamo came first in 1960, and among the trivia reported as the expensive fiasco began was that Duke wouldn't hear of portable septic-tank johns when the huge company set up location on a ranch of several hundred acres outside of Brackettville, Texas, close to the Mexican border. Five miles of piping were laid to facilitate the installation of modern plumbing that flushed.

In the movie circles of London and Rome, where Duke's name still provokes shudders, that must have come as quite a surprise to the Italian and British crew who had the misfortune to work the Libyan location of *Legend of the Lost* in 1958, a Batjac production, produced, I guess by Duke and director Henry Hathaway. Sophia Loren and Rossano Brazzi were the costars, making it eligible for Italian government subsidy and status as a co-production.

All the preliminary work, the selection of the location at Ghadames, an oasis situated at the center of an ancient camel route leading to Tripoli and the sea, had been organized by Duke's production crew. If they consulted either the Italians or Libyans they employed to assist in the preparation of the production, there were no signs of it. The whole affair was a mess, from start to finish, an American-made mess.

Duke, Hathaway and the American crew proceeded to organize the desert location as though it were something put together by old Nat Levine for one of his serials. Although Europe is famed from the Baltic to the Mediterranean for its camping equipment, Batjac Productions shipped a boat load of surplus Army junk from Hollywood to Genoa, thence to Tripoli where a tent city was built—resembling the Hoovervilles of the depression. The tents were shabby, stained, full of holes. The septic toilets were too small and too few. Once they were installed the showers functioned erratically leaving half a dozen soap-covered men to make out as best they could until water pressure resumed—sometimes, the following day.

Maybe not much more was to be expected from a desert, but down the road a bit, at one of the oil companies, French business men had created a beautiful tent city containing tents with sliding doors and johns that flushed when you whistled at them.

But to make matters worse, Batjac had shipped the kind of food that suited the particular tastes of the Americans—hundreds of cans of pork and beans, cases of pickled onions, corned beef, corned beef hash, canned potatoes, canned tomatoes, tons of pancake mix and cans of maple syrup, corn flakes, canned corn. And canned American coffee.

The Arabs refused to eat the canned stuff, fearing it might contain pork. Italians loathe corn and demanded *pasta*. No one wanted anything to do with pickled onions or the corned beef hash. And everyone, including Americans who worked abroad, despised American coffee which lost its famous reputation during World War II.

There was a threat of a strike unless more suitable food was provided and camp conditions improved. Duke and his men couldn't understand the resentment. Weren't they Americans feeding and housing underpriviledged Arabs, Italians, and English?

A new cooking staff was installed but when an

emergency arose the doctor in charge of the company's health refused to perform minor surgery under existing conditions. He had filled his tent with every medicine known to man; still he insisted the patient be flown to Tripoli for treatment.

On location, miles away from the camp site, Sophia was found crying. No toilet facility had been provided in her dressing room trailer—nor for the other women on the set, Sophia's hairdresser and the script girl. Duke's men were surly when told of this—as they were about everything involving relations between the Americans and the Italians and Arabs. The last two were always referred to as "they" as were Sophia and the two women, "Why can't *they* use the sand—like the rest of us?" was the answer. An accomodation, however, was made the next day.

Wayne was surprised by the reaction to his tent city—and to the complaints of the "foreign" crew. In his mind's eye he was giving them a break—work, three meals a day and they were beefing? The American attitude of Duke's "boys" was characteristic hard-hat, "Well, if *they* don't like it, why don't *they* go home? Who needs *them*?" No one considered that they were employing skilled studio technicians, most of them capable in French, English, their own language, of course and even, some Arabic. They had grace and manners, —besides being tough, hard-working men, every inch the match of the Hollywood craftsmen.

The response of Duke and Hathaway to every

163

mishap was petulant and snarling. Everyone was stupid—except themselves.

You had the feeling that Wayne, obsessed with his "tough" image expected the same from everyone else—that, for a few bucks a week, everyone was supposed to be "tough" too. And if you didn't like it—there was always Russia.

Yep, there was always Russia. And England too for when Duke badly needed a helicopter to get some aerial shots of the Tuaregs riding across the desert astride their camels in their blue veils—one of the great visual scenes in the picture—even super-American Duke Wayne couldn't wheedle a helicopter out of Wheeler Air Base. The U.S. brass there claimed it would be flying outside their range of control for helicopters! But the British came through. They cheerily provided a chopper, a pilot to operate it—and no one at Whitehall seemed disturbed. The British blokes, a mere handful compared to the hundreds of Americans at Wheeler, came to watch the shooting, and it turned into quite a jolly day—and evening. One of the few pleasant memories *Legend of the Lost* left behind in the Libyan desert.

* * *

Perhaps, remembering that winter of discontent of *Legend of the Lost*, Duke had profited from the experience and was determined not to repeat his old mistakes in filming *The Alamo*.

The movie had been the dream of his career and to film it, he had laid down everything he owned, hocked his interest in his independent company, raised capital everywhere he could find it. Financial support of the picture had been turned down by Herbert Yates, which precipitated Duke's break with Republic, and a host of other producers, men for whom Duke had made millions.

It was sad in a way. Wayne had done more for Republic than the studio could ever repay. Besides his own name he had brought in top talent like John Ford and Frank Borzage. He had shared Yates' dream of building Republic into a major— and time after time had gone far afield from his own contract to help out. But it wasn't in the cards.

Wayne played Davy Crockett and directed *The Alamo* saying, "We wanted to create a moment in history that will show this generation of Americans what their country stands for." It was a big big picture in every sense of the word and because John Ford made a few visits to the location, it was erroneously assumed that he'd directed *The Alamo* between scenes.

That *The Alamo* was a hundred percent artistic flop is incorrect. It did get knocked by the Eastern elitists, but the reviews praised Wayne's handling of the action sequences. It wasn't so much the so-so reviews that knocked down the picture's commercial value as the exploitation that seemed to bother people, the intimidating tone of the ads, the inference that you weren't patriotic if you didn't pay your three bucks to see *The Alamo*. These ideas were the creation of an old Hollywood master of ballyhoo, Russell Birdwell, a genius at grabbing attention, vulgar when it came to taste.

165

Duke had been taken, and it wasn't the first time. He'd become the typical Hollywood provincial, the man who honestly believed in the supreme talent of the men surrounding him, entrusting *The Alamo* to a likeable but passé flack linked to the old Hollywood.

Duke put in five tough years working off the debts incurred by *The Alamo* and then in 1964 Duke got the news; he had cancer and would lose a lung. Because so much rides on a star's health, insurance, contracts, commitments, secrecy is the standard operating procedure when someone of Duke's importance is hospitalized. Hollywood seethed with rumors and his representatives sought to calm the press with non-committal statements. Eventually reporters got at the truth and Duke, characteristically, began taking the press—and his fans—into his confidence. He was frank about his cancer as L.B.J. had been about his operation.

Told to rest for six months, Pilar managed to keep him quiet for about six weeks. He gave up smoking, started smoking again, cut down to a pack a day, turned to chewing gum, tried a pipe, and, being a tough guy, chawed plug.

* * *

The Green Berets came three years later. In the meantime Duke had reassured the public and himself (partially) that he had licked the Big C. In a sense, he had. Duke was alive and that he rightly considered a miracle. But he was incapable of resting and relaxing as he'd been warned by his doctor.

They needed morale builders in Vietnam badly and because of his health no one had asked Wayne before. But when his recovery seemed evident, he was asked to fly over and repeat what he'd done in World War II—slap together some kind of routine and then sit down and talk to the kids. It was the kind of assignment Duke knew well and always handled beautifully. The man packs enormous charm.

The result of that front-line encounter with dispirited Americans involved in a war they couldn't understand was *The Green Berets*. Duke came back feeling he had to tell the story—although, like Goldwater, he believed the whole Vietnam business could be disposed of by massive bombings of the enemy, even if it involved atomic force.

Wayne dragged himself through the production of *The Green Berets*, playing a role poorly suited to his age. But the picture needed the quality he would bring it. It was propaganda pure and simple—the only movie made glorifying the Vietnam War. Duke was alone. He stood on his convictions. He made the film against everyone's advice.

The reaction had to be expected under the circumstances, and criticism went far beyond the circle of the Eastern Establishment. The reviews were brutal in New York, but they were brutal elsewhere. New Yorkers didn't bother to picket when *The Green Berets* was shown—but they did elsewhere—even in Middle America.

John Wayne had taken the second and the most unnecessary beating of his professional career. But this time he showed more maturity and settled matters by confining retaliatory statements to simple declarative sentences. "I felt the movie needed to be done. I still think it's a damned fine show."

True Grit came right along in 1969—proving Duke led a charmed life and no matter how he antagonized people or how those damned sophisticated folks back East antagonized him, there was always another piece of pie in the sky for the Duke to reach up and grab. *True Grit* was certainly it, and it didn't matter if the writer, Charles Portis, had Duke in mind when he sat down to write his novel about Rooster Cogburn, a "mean old bastard, a one-eyed, whiskey-soaked, sloppy old son-of-a-bitch just like me"—as Duke explained it. Writing novels with mental images of movie character actors is an old writer's trick. And Portis was just playing it cool—grateful for the big movie sale and the smash hit Duke made of it.

Old friend Henry Hathaway, with his whining voice and constant complaining, dragged the performance of his career out of Duke. As Rooster he's too old, too mean and too tired for any of the feats expected by a girl who has hired him to find the killer of her father. But Duke and Rooster blended into one, played out the heroics, lacing them with whiskey, action and brilliance, as Rooster brought the villains to justice.

Once more, to sum up his appraisal of Wayne, biographer Alan Barbour turned to the Eastern Establishment. Wrote Barbour, "William Wolf of *Cue Magazine*, not always the kindest of reviewers, said of Wayne's performance, "When the John Wayne retrospects are in full swing, this will loom as one of his finest movie triumphs. Wayne steals the film in the role of tough colorful Rooster Cogburn".

His fans agreed and the Academy gave him the Oscar. Most actors would have called it quits then, but not Duke. He went right on, making a half dozen more before he teamed up with Katharine Hepburn for *Rooster Cogburn*, a further adventure of the hard-drinking, hair-trigger marshal.

The co-starring of the two legends was considered important enough for the event to be recorded on television where Katie, asked why she'd never appeared with Duke before, answered simply, "He never asked me."

The review of the picture in *Time Magazine* said it all: "Wayne and Hepburn have outlived the cleverness and malice of critics and commentators. They have accumulated such tremendous energy of personality and survival that they outface such shattering pigmies by their mere presence. This presence is not so 'mere'—it is also our presence. There is something exhilarating and disturbing about watching the great long-lived movie stars in their last films, perhaps even more so today when we are strangely out of touch with older people...So it is almost pointless to complain that *Rooster Cogburn* doesn't do justice to its stars. Almost, but not quite. The only reason to see this movie is to witness this gentle collision of two larger-than-life people who have spent their lives as professional incarnations of our fantasies, and who have earned the right to be incarnations of themselves."

* * *

Since *True Grit*, Wayne pictures have not been the sure-fire draws they once were which doesn't exactly warrant classifying them as failures. There's such a thing as a "Wayne gross" and both producers and exhibitors have known it so long they take it for granted. In 1975 Wayne dropped out of the first ten in the exhibitors' poll for the first time since he began heading it. Now he rates fifteenth—which isn't exactly a disgrace and would cause someone like Roddy MacDowell or Joel Grey to jump with joy.

The Wayne compound is at Newport by the sea. The Duke lives in a large, cheery house and there are celebrations throughout the year when all the children assemble with their wives, husbands and grandchildren. These, for Duke, who had so little time for his family when he was younger, are moments of great joy.

Pilar lives in a house nearby. They speak to each other daily on the telephone. How often they meet is their secret. The couple separated in 1973, and various reasons have been advanced for the break-up. "Other women" of course. Then, they say Pilar got weary of all the demands made on her—that being a movie wife suited a certain period of their life—but it had become inconsistent with Duke's age and his health. She wanted him to settle down. She fought the long hard battle that led him to quit cigarette smoking. And there's much more Pilar could take credit for.

But speculation remains just that—speculation. Among the Wayne wives, Pilar gave all the appearances of the jackpot, the tough one, determined to survive. Besides being pretty, she was bright and intelligent. She was able to influence Duke. She quieted him down when that fabled temper started to flare. But the truth is clear—they are apart and, at this writing at least, there seems little liklihood of a reconciliation. But odds are that Pilar won't relinquish her claim on Duke until she's convinced no other course is open to her. She once said, "Maybe we were destined to live apart, and yet remain in love."

And what's next on the Wayne agenda? No retirement certainly. That's a dirty word around the Wayne compound. Especially after *True Grit* and *Rooster Cogburn.* Could they mean the beginning of a whole new career for the stormy old man who's done about everything in the movies—but become a great character star? Who knows? Wayne has never been predictable, and now is not the time for gypsy seers to peer into his future.

Age is the enemy—and the condition of his health. Regardless of how he has bluffed his way through the past decade, the years can not have been comfortable or reassuring. Still, to count him out is way, way premature.

Wayne won't buy that—and the chances are

even that he'll manage a few more spectaculars yet—not to cheat the guy with the scythe—but, perhaps, to have a few more snarls at the Eastern establishment.

For all hands, East and West, that would be a good thing. Better a snarling, battling curmudgeon like Wayne to have lived with, gotten angry with—and enjoyed—than one of those actors they end up describing as a man who never did anything wrong.

Duke's right when he says he's lasted so long as a popular actor because he was lucky in getting good directors, and stories that had something. No one ever went out of the theatre disappointed.

As Duke says, "It was all right to pay twenty-five cents, wasn't it? Remember?"

PART FOUR

Gary Cooper

There are clues in Cooper's films that often have mirrored our democratic mood if not our nature. He was the hero of "A Farewell to Arms" when we were preoccupied with pacifism, the liberal-minded Mr. Deeds in the New Deal era, and both Robert Jordan (civilian turned guerrilla) and Sergeant York (pacifist turned warrior) in a world at war. He was a lonely hero in "High Noon" at the beginning of the Eisenhower era. In his thirty-six years as a public figure, Gary Cooper was the sort of American other Americans would like somehow to have been.

*T*he Picture was *For Whom the Bell Tolls.*
*A*kim Tamiroff was a Russian actor with a thick accent, wide expressive face and eyes that told a situation in a glance. He possessed a bag of scene-stealing tricks that put other masters of the art to shame. After his first scenes in the Hemingway drama of the Spanish Civil War with Gary Cooper were finished, Tamiroff excitedly attended the rushes, looking forward to the grandness of his characterization as one of a valiant band of Loyalists holding a key mountain pass against the enemy. Tamiroff took his reputation for theatrical larceny seriously.

As the rushes were screened, two or three times as usual, Tamiroff became increasingly depressed. Leaving the projection room he held tightly onto a friend's arm, "It's impossible. There's nothing you can do. It's always Cooper. You never look at anyone else. Not even me. Who looks at Bergman yet, when he's on the screen?"

The late James Agee called Cooper a "male beauty"—an opinion shared by director Josef von Sternberg. Sternberg's camera zoomed in on Cooper as carefully and as sensuously as it did on von Sternberg's own creation, Marlene Dietrich, in Coop's first smash hit, *Morocco*. The camera literally caressed his perfect features and lingered provocatively as it ran down his lean, lanky, well-muscled body. Cooper was the phallic symbol of the drama—the male beauty the rest of the action was played against.

It didn't stop there. When Gary was having his wildly publicized affair with Clara Bow, the "It Girl," they called him the "It Boy." When he first came to Paramount, Coop worked so hard he often slept at the studio, dozed during the day. The crew dubbed him "The Sleeping Beauty."

It was impossible to photograph Cooper from a wrong angle, and this perfection of features lasted almost until the end of his career. Maturity added to his attractiveness, creating a durable charm.

Audiences took to him instantly and by the time Coop officially reached stardom, few movie fans were unaware that he was six feet, 2½ inches tall, weighed 175 pounds, regardless of how much food he downed, had blue eyes and was enjoyed as much by male audiences as by the women who had started swooning over him long before *Morocco*. Had Coop been a longshoreman he might well have been the most popular man at the waterfront bars. Had he been at Yale he might have been the guy voted "most popular man in his class." Since he went to Hollywood and became an actor, he became someone vastly more important—the quintessential movie actor, admired and envied by those he looked upon as his betters. "We try, but he *is*," Charles Laughton admitted. "In his heart he is pure," John Barrymore said. "He believes in it."

George Cukor put it more clearly, "A really sincere actor with very few tricks—someone like Gary Cooper—is dismissed with 'Oh, but he's such a simple person, what he is playing is so simple.' Look at it right up close, it is much more than that."

There was nothing simple about Gary Cooper, either in his art or his private life—even if audiences recall him best as the gallant hero of a dozen-odd great Western movies, one actor who meant it when he said that old cliche, "When you call me that, smile." Beyond the cowboy there lay a talented, complicated man, an actor who embraced a wide variety of roles, playing them with distinction—a Britisher in *Lives of a Bengal Lancer*, a small-town American in *Mr. Deeds Goes to Town*, a white-tied socialite in *Bluebeard's Eighth Wife* and Lou Gehrig of the Bronx in *The Pride of the Yankees*, which won him his first Oscar. A triumph came toward the end of his career when he played the lined, worn sheriff of *High Noon*, generally considered one of the finest Westerns ever made and Cooper's best performance.

As most actors do, Cooper brought some of himself to each role he played, for Coop was anything but the laconic "yep" and "nope" man the public imagined him. This taciturnity was a defense mechanism against intrusion into his private world. Coop actually was a great talker who spoke with wit and intelligence about a lot of things. Said playwright Clifford Odets, "He knew all about oceans and tides. He had the enthusiasms of a boy. He had an old-fashioned politeness, but he said nothing casually." When Cooper met Pablo Picasso in France he said, "You're a hell of a guy, but I don't really get your pictures." The great artist was delighted. "That doesn't matter," Picasso said, "If you really want to do something for me, get me one of those hats you wear in the movies." Picasso (who got the hat and sent Coop a painting) was not alone in being charmed by Cooper's directness and his refusal to be what he was not.

He was a great sleeper; he could tilt back his hat, lean back in a chair and drop off between takes of the most demanding picture. He was a man who enjoyed the simple sensation of being out of doors; he was a hunter, a skier, a skin diver who found almost mystic satisfaction in the ocean depths. He collected sporting guns and not only loved automobiles but insisted on washing his favorite cars himself.

No matter how many things occupied him in later years his career came first. The Cooper image was as carefully guarded as the gold at Fort Knox, but Coop always had time for the ladies. The romantic side of his private world was every bit as exciting and dramatic as the characters in his more than eighty-five pictures.

Most actors depend on studio publicity departments to build up images as sex symbols. True, Coop, in the early days, enjoyed the help of studio trumpeteers, but his romantic capers gave them plenty of material to work with—genuine stuff, not synthetic "whispered about, it's rumored kind of gossip."

* * *

The most common legend about Cooper was that he came to the screen fresh off the range, a virgin cowboy who wandered into all that fame and fortune by accident. The legend had nothing to do with the facts, except that he was born in Helena, Montana, and his father did own a small cattle ranch where he learned to ride, shoot and punch cows. His father, Charles Henry Cooper, was a lawyer from Bedfordshire, England who came to Helena and decided to stay in America. Gary was born May 7, 1901. When he was nine years old, the Coopers moved to England where, for four years, he attended the Dunstable School, a good sound "public" school, which, in British English, means a private school for the upper or middle classes.

Coop lowered his dignity by having a fist fight with a newsboy. Apart from that, life in England was serene enough and, with war clouds hovering over Europe, the Coopers returned to Montana, the older Cooper feeling he had no right to involve his American wife and son in what he appeared then to be a purely European dispute.

When America entered World War I, Coop, too young for military service, did the only ranch work of his life. Because of the shortage of help, Coop got up every morning at the ranch, milked the cows and attended a variety of chores before heading off to his senior years in high school.

Then he went to Wesleyan College in Helena and studied at Grinnell College in Iowa for three years. There were times when he thought he wanted to be a surgeon, but his major interest was in cartooning, born of drawing classes in high school. Samples of his work show that Coop would never have made it as a cartoonist, and a man who enjoyed sleep as he did would hardly have qualified as the most reliable of surgeons.

Cooper, Sr. went on to the Montana Supreme Court, leaving it in 1924 to return to private practice. Coop, now on his own, had given dramatics a try at college but was turned down. And in his home town cartooning failed to impress local newspaper editors. So he hung around the Cooper ranch, punching cattle for his father, plainly bored at the way his life was shaping up. He headed for Chicago, hoping for an opening in commercial art. That attempt got nowhere. It was winter and his father was in Los Angeles working on a case involving the estate of one of his Montana clients. Coop decided that if he was going to starve to death, it was better to do it in a warmer climate, closer to people he knew. So he got himself to L.A. and back into the world of his mother's cooking.

In 1956, in a story titled *Well, It Was This Way,* Coop told George Scullin of the *Saturday Evening Post,* of the accidental meeting that got him into the movies: "On a fine December day in 1925, I walked down Hollywood Boulevard. Near Vine Street I saw coming toward me a couple of sorry-looking cowhands. They were beat up. They looked as though they had raced a stampede and lost, but seeing me, they brightened up.

" 'Boy, howdy.' said one. 'If it isn't Slim!' 'You sure look gaunt, fellah,' said the other.

"I looked over the bruised cheekbones, the black eyes and torn clothes and the cowboy hats...they were Jimmy Galen and Jimmy Calloway. Boyhood friends from Montana. They were lawyers' sons, same as me, but when I last heard of them they were riding broncs in a rodeo."

They told Coop that the rodeo show had gone broke, and they'd ended up in Hollywood. Instead of wrestling steers they were paid to fall off horses in the movies. They were stunt men. "What a snap!" they told Coop. They were making ten dollars a day.

The two old friends helped Coop get his first job as a stunt man—after overcoming the director's objections to the clothes he was wearing. They hailed "Slim" as Montana's greatest ever, as though a super-breed of horses needed to be invented just for him to ride.

"And that's the way it was," continued Coop. "My friends had got me the job, and in those days the average Western was shot in about ten days. But that didn't mean the extras worked all those days. Usually we would hold up all the stagecoaches, shoot all the bandits, fight off all the Indians and wreck all the saloons in one fast day and that was it.

"The next day out we'd be in the sand dunes as the French Foreign Legion, holding off the Arabs in another picture. After a week of that you didn't need rest so much as hospitalization."

It wasn't too tough for a tall, lean handsome guy like Coop to pick up work. He was a good rider and roper. Westerns were the stock in trade of Hollywood, and the mechanics were simple. Assistant directors and casting directors quickly knew the reliable members of the extra fraternity and Cooper started getting regular work.

After six months Coop reached a peak—an Indian fighter with Richard Dix, a Cossack with Valentino, an outlaw conspiring against Tom Mix. He was always the one who took the tumble, fell into a gulch and got shot from a galloping horse. Being close enough to Tom Mix to see that his publicity was all true—that he made $17,000 a week, lived in a beautiful home, drove several cars, made Coop decide to do something about becoming an actor. It was the only avenue open to save his neck. A stunt man's life was profitable—but far from healthy.

Oddly, one of the reasons Coop had become such a good rider was because of an early accident. He went through the canvas top of a Model-T in a crackup. There were no broken bones but he'd torn

Gary Cooper was Hollywood's Golden Boy—the male beauty loved by many beautiful women.

some hip ligaments and was advised to stay in bed.

Coop hated the confinement and prevailed on his father to let him go to the ranch where instead of hobbling around on painful crutches he eased around on a gentle colt. Until then Coop said he'd been an ordinary slam-bang rodeo type rider. Now he learned to understand and anticipate a horse's movements instinctively, even at full gallop. Any time he was surprised by the horse, he'd feel a twinge in his hip. That taught him alertness, and in a few weeks he was riding with an ease that he confessed "No amount of training could have given me."

Actually, years later, Coop discovered that he'd broken his hip in the car accident—that it had never really healed, just filled in somehow. Doctors marvelled, on looking at X-rays, why the young man hadn't been crippled for life instead of being one of the finest horsemen in movies.

* * *

Who discovered Gary Cooper depends on whose biography you read and wisely Coop never singled out any of the three who claimed the honor. They were all good friends for many years and if they wanted kudos for discovering Hollywood's Beautiful Golden Boy, he wasn't inclined to disappoint any of them. That was how he played things.

Coop took the first step himself by sending photographs to the studios and producers showing him in a variety of poses, modelled after the favorites of the day, Francis X. Bushman, John

Barrymore, Valentino. That got him nothing but more jobs as stunt man. Then he decided to make his own screen test. It represented an investment—renting a horse, for one thing. The test showed off Coop's riding skill, then patting the horse in affectionate farewell to cut down the rental. Coop performed some stunts, like leaping a fence, rolling around on the ground after fake falls, brushing himself off and for the finale whipping off his hat as he faced the camera in a big close-up of the Cooper grin.

Coop lugged his precious can of film from studio to studio and it almost got him a good part at Paramount. He took the test to Samuel Goldwyn's studio as production was about to start on *The Winning Of Barbara Worth* costarring one of the magical teams of the silents, Ronald Colman and Vilma Banky. The second lead was a possible, and Goldwyn tentatively approved him. This gave Goldwyn his stake in Cooper's future. The part of Abe Lee contained two good scenes; one in which Abe saves Colman's life; the other, a death scene in which he expires in Colman's arms.

When Herold Goodwin. who was set for the picture, couldn't make it, director King Vidor, who had Cooper standing by as a cowboy extra, dirtied him up and gave him a crack at the part. There's the doubtful legend that Cooper's casting dismayed Colman and Banky who feared the brash newcomer would steal the picture. He didn't quite manage that but Vidor was able to say thereafter that he'd given Coop his first real break.

Which leads up to the story most old-timers

around Hollywood believe. There were few smarter women working around the studios than scenarist Frances Marion whose influence went far beyond the scripts she wrote. There was vast respect for anything Frances suggested. Others snorted, but Louis B. Mayer listened when Frances suggested years later that Marie Dressler be brought out of obscurity—and near poverty—for *Anna Christie*, Garbo's first talkie, promising L.B. "she'll make a mint of money for you."

At any rate, as Miss Marion wrote in her memoirs, she was asked by a friend to look at Cooper's test. The writer spotted him sitting in the waiting room and knew, before the test unwound, that he was right for the part. She got Goldwyn to look at it—and *Barbara Worth* altered Gary Cooper's career.

Although Samuel Goldwyn wanted Cooper, liked him personally and thought he'd acquitted himself admirably in *Barbara Worth*, the producer was honest enough to admit in later years that he couldn't imagine in Coop in any but Western roles. Goldwyn didn't go in heavily for sage-brush movies, so the best he could offer in the way of a contract was $65 a week. Paramount countered with a deal that offered Coop starring roles in a series of Zane Grey Westerns and the promise of parts in other pictures at $400 a week. Coop grabbed it.

Coop knew exactly what to do with his money. He'd seen enough of the good life in Hollywood to want a piece of it. He bought himself a snappy red roadster, started to acquire a wardrobe and moved in with a buddy in one of those neat, little bungalow courts smothered in geranium plants that were the pride of old Hollywood.

Now, it's unlikely that at the age of twenty-five, looking more like a young god than a movie stunt man, that Coop hadn't slipped in and out of any number of Hollywood pull-down beds before *Barbara Worth*. However, the private lives of stunt men from Montana weren't exactly bandied about, because no one really cared, but after Coop played a second lead to Colman, he became someone to buzz about. People discovered that his real name was Frank James Cooper, that he'd changed it to Gary on the advice of a female agent who came from Gary, Indiana, which was the least of her problems compared to the terrible crush she had on Coop.

She wasn't alone in sighing herself to sleep every night with Coop on her mind. There were quite a few young men around Hollywood with the same wistful look in their eyes whenever they got close to that long, blue-eyed cowpoke from Montana.

Coop's roommate, like the budding star, was an extra and bit player around town, eager to drop out of the scene when Coop landed his contract just to become Coop's "gofer", to wash the car, run the house, do the errands and keep his friend comfortable and satisfied. As far as Coop was concerned the arrangement was working out beautifully because if any young fellow needed a "slavey" it was Coop—personal reasons aside.

Paramount decided it had bought a winner

cheap and the best way to shape him up was to toss him from picture to picture. The studio began shooting Cooper pictures in pairs, working him both day and night. In the first half of 1927, six Gary Cooper pictures were released—at the rate of one a month. You couldn't really call them "Cooper pictures." The real star was *Flash, the Wonder Horse.*

In *Nevada*, Cooper was the hero who rescued Thelma Todd from the villainous William Powell. Thelma, at her blonde loveliest, turned to him one day, "That's your enemy," she said, pointing to the camera. "Never forget it. It doesn't lie. Everything you feel goes right into that lens." Years later Coop recalled Thelma's remark as the best acting lesson he had ever gotten from anyone—indeed the only acting lesson.

Clara Bow was top doll on the Paramount lot and what Clara saw and wanted—Clara got. She asked the studio to cast young Cooper opposite her in *Children of Divorce* but the studio compromised by giving him a short role as a reporter, and it took more than two dozen takes before the scene worked. Coop's career never looked less promising, but, as always in crucial moments in his life, there was a woman lurking in the background. Two women, as a matter of fact, Clara herself and busybody Hedda Hopper.

Hedda was an actress in those days, one of these mediocrities you could never say was either good or bad. She had a strident style that suited the kind of role she usually played, the smart, beautifully groomed cat ready to bad mouth anyone within hearing distance.

When Hedda became a columnist years later she

liked to recall the triumphs that had taken place earlier—when, to read her, she was one of the most sought-after actresses in Hollywood, darting from picture to picture like a fluttery butterfly. She was proud of the couples she brought together—especially Clara Bow and Gary Cooper. Hedda had a supporting role in *Children of Divorce*.

Realizing that Clara was smitten with Coop, she urged the tiny redhead to go after him and let him know what was on her mind. Evidently Clara did and, although director Frank Lloyd wanted to bounce Coop off the picture several times, Clara's clout kept him on the job long enough for them to get friendly and to start making news in the columns. Inevitably, the studio capitalized on the "love affair" by teaming the young stars in *It*—the title Clara had been given when Eleanor Glyn visited Hollywood.

Then, according to Hedda, she took Coop aside, explained the harm his roommate was doing to his reputation, and that it would be best to get out of the situation and play around with Clara. It was one of those conversations when Coop chose to say neither "yep" or "nope"—but simply walked away.

Hedda Hopper's homophobia would some day cost her a bundle when, in one of her books, she insisted, against everyone's advice, from her publisher's lawyers to agents, on including a paragraph libelling Liz Taylor's second husband, Michael Wilding, as a homosexual, claiming he had shared digs—and a relationship—with another prominent actor before coming to Hollywood and marrying Liz. Hedda paid an out-of-court settlement of a suit brought by Wilding and she was never the same again. The case, with its humiliation and reflection on her personal stability and credibility as a columnist began the physical decline of an elderly woman once considered indestructible.

If she were around today, anti-establishment publications would label Hedda as the worst species of *fag hag*—women who associate with gays because of age or their inability to find satisfaction in their own personal lives. Hedda's newspaper career thrived on exploiting homosexuals—gays who supplied her with a steady stream of inside stories from within the studios. One, notoriously bitchy, was instrumental in persuading Hedda to call the Wilding shot as she wanted to. Hedda disregarded the very basis of newspapering—corroborative evidence to support an accusation. For escorts, Hedda invariably leaned heavily on the company of gay young men, yet she never missed an opportunity to snipe at their life style.

The "long ago" incident of Coop and his "roomie" wasn't altogether a secret, but it was virtually forgotten when Hopper chose to resurrect it to dramatize her importance, and to claim credit for the synthetic Gary Cooper—Clara Bow romance.

That was Hedda—a Medusa of little intelligence and no taste, a cruel and vicious victim of her own frustrations. Herself asexual, her jollies evidently were derived from vicarious intimacy with the foibles of others. Only Hedda would have printed Liz Taylor's answer about her affair with Eddie

Marlene Dietrich, Lupe Velez, Clara Bow—all were close to Coop in those early years.

Fisher, "Hedda, you don't expect me to sleep alone, do you?"

An underground gossip would have taken that for granted. But Hedda, terribly afraid, took nothing for granted—not her fame, power or her money. She pointed to the handsome $200,000 Benedict Canyon house her column had built and spoke her tragic epitaph, "That's the house that fear built."

But the era of Hedda's reign of fear was still to come as Clara and Coop made the rounds together. He was romancing in the big leagues, and his name and face were spread all over the fan magazines and Sunday sections of newspapers—where publicity counted in those days. Fans really had a hand in making stars. Big studios like Paramount counted the bags of mail as they came in and the autographed photographs that went out.

The publicity was enough to warrant Coop's casting in *Wings*, an exciting air epic starring Richard Arlen and Buddy Rogers. Coop had only one brief scene to score in—as a flier going out to meet his death. The combination of William Wellman's direction and Coop's growing awareness of how to deal with "the enemy, the camera" made it a standout.

In the manner of manufactured Hollywood romances, the Clara Bow—Cooper affair dwindled away and Coop sheepishly told the fan magazines "it wasn't such a big thing after all"—and no one recorded the fiery red-head's response. Clara's career was already on the wane—it was briefly spectacular but beyond tiny Clara's buoyance and vitality lay little real talent. With talkies she faded into obscurity, a marriage to Rex Bell, once a secondary cowboy star, who became a Nevada politician, and finally, there was Clara's long, lonely battle against mental disorders and cancer. But Clara was a charmer until very near the end— every Christmas her old Hollywood friends heard from her with cheery greetings, affirming hope in the future and her won recovery.

* * *

When Lupe Velez and Gary Cooper looked each other over as they met on the set of *Wolf Song*, the explosion from the Paramount lot could be heard miles away in the Hollywood Hills—even if most of the dynamite went off inside Lupe. She was a lady who made decisions quickly, and Coop was hers— not only for the duration of the picture, but as long as she could hold him.

This inspired some wild publicity about a nude swimming sequence that promised to perk up things considerably in *Wolf Song* but, like all such scenes, it was filmed in long shot and turned out nothing more than a "little yawn".

While publicity men fed items to the press about the "new twosome," in the vernacular of the day, top Paramount brass fumed. To them, Coop was still a simon-pure cowboy doing Zane Grey things—even if they magnanimously tossed him a crumb now and then away from the stable. They weren't nearly as afraid of the publicity—that was okay—but, knowing Lupe, a lot better than Coop did, they feared their Golden Boy might one Saturday evening be lured to Tijuana and marriage. While any marriage of a young romantic lead was discouraged as a matter of policy—a union of all-American Coop with a Mexican hot pepper like Lupe might help sell enchiladas but would shatter the popcorn business in neighborhood theatres catering to young Western audiences.

Lupe was an irresistible bundle of loveliness—a free and uninhibited soul who flung herself into life and life with abandon. When she laughed and shook that mass of raven locks it was like seeing a lovely child that you wanted to pick up and carry home on the spot. Even the women who huffed, puffed and snorted about Lupe's free and easy ways, her habit of embracing and kissing everybody on sight, found it difficult to really say anything unkind about her. Lupe was that rarest of Hollywood rarities—a girl universally loved.

She went bra-less long before Jean Harlow was heard of, explaining that "it allowed the body to breathe." And what a body! I met it once, at the Palace theatre in New York where she was making a personal appearance, opening the dressing room door as she often did, stark naked. I was about eleven or twelve, taken backstage by a friend.

Lupe was a Latin Clara Bow, which may have explained Coop's attraction to her—but much brighter and vastly more talented. She was a fine comedienne but, when it was needed, could manage a dramatic scene convincingly. She was always sure of herself—explaining that was because she prayed a lot. God was very important to Lupe—and Coop, who later converted to Catholicism, had his first if somewhat unusual exposure to the religion through Lupe.

Her devotion to God and her church was fervent and real, but there were times when the Mexican Spitfire became the despair of pastors in Los Angeles who would be awakened at all hours of the night and early morning by Lupe banging on the doors of their churches or parish houses screaming, "Open up. Open up. When Lupe want to pray, Lupe pray. Why you close church doors? Church is God's House—for Lupe and everybody else. For the whole world."

And it was pretty much the same, when it came to Coop, "When Lupe love," she told reporters, "Lupe love."

Lupe kept Coop on a tight leash for as long as she held him. She thought nothing of breaking into his apartment at night—no more than she did of wakening the priests—to make sure he wasn't entertaining another woman. Lupe lived in the Hollywood Hills and Coop presented her with an eagle as a gag. Lupe fell in love with the eagle, decided it was lonely and needed a mate. For weeks thereafter when Coop and Lupe entertained, guests were disarmed by the pair of screaming eagles.

Lupe's, like Clara Bow's, was another broken heart in the parade of women that swiftly and surely led Gary Cooper to fame. If ever there was a star who, in many senses, was created by the women who loved him, Gary Cooper was the man. One by one the pieces began fitting together; Frances Marion, the woman who discovered him; Clara Bow, the gal who helped him to his first romantic leads and put his name in the fan magazines, and Lupe Velez whose infatuation for her tall handsome lover made him seem to be the most explosive man in the world.

It was all choreographed beautifully—even to the spectacular diFrasso affair. A middle-aged woman, Countess Dorothy diFrasso flipped for Gary beginning in 1930. The Countess, born Dorothy Taylor to a glove manufacturer in Rochester, New York, shared an inheritance with her brother, a New York stock broker, who enlarged it into a tidy fortune. Dorothy became one of the first Americans of the Roaring Twenties to buy herself a title by way of marriage to an impoverished Roman nobleman, giving her title to his villa as well. She became an international cafe socialite, alternating between Rome, Venice for the Cole Porter season and Paris for nights at Bricktop's. The Prince of Wales, the cream of European society and theatrical darlings like Clifton Webb, Libby Holman, Helen Morgan and Marilyn Miller gathered there for the interval before the Deauville racing season and the summer at Biarritz. As a mature and experienced connoisseur of male pulchritude, no one was surprised when the Countess suddenly began adding Hollywood to her itinerary, beginning with visits as the houseguest of Hollywood's Royal Couple, Mary Pickford and Douglas Fairbanks.

They reigned at an estate named Pickfair, and no available stud ever rejected an invitation, any more than he would turn down a Command Performance or a visit to the White House. So the chunky lady with all the jewels and money in the bank was able to assess the available talent from the best possible vantage point. If there were an award for predatory female of the season, Dorothy would have been collecting trophies for years. There was a hardness to her face reflecting the anxiety she'd put into the job of ensnaring males, but she could be an exceedingly pleasant woman, cultured to a degree, able to turn the charm on and off at will. What these qualities and her really beautiful milk-white skin didn't accomplish, her pocketbook would. Dorothy never thought twice about laying green on the line when that was the language best understood.

Dorothy flipped over Coop and the time seemed right for Coop to flip back. Hollywood took the new couple in stride—the town had seen more bizarre sights than the puffy, jaded *Contessa* all atwitter about her tall, raw-boned, young discovery, a silent, blue-eyed, fresh beauty plucked from the plains of Montana.

Like one of Lupe's eagles she swooped down upon him, talons extended, ready to claw anyone who got near him. She couldn't wait to tote her cowboy back to Europe to dangle him before her friends and teach him which fork went with which salad. Fortunately, Coop's plans were flexible.

Having been offered a raise by Paramount from $400 to $600 a week, Coop wasn't sure that the amount was consistent with his rapidly growing fan constituency. Paramount had promised exhibitors four Cooper pictures for the 1930-31 season. Coop figured if he was being offered as bait, he deserved more money. So he accepted Dorothy's invitation—becoming Tarzan to her Jane as they sailed for Europe.

Once abroad, the Contessa paraded the lanky actor through the chic *boites*, the grand ballrooms of Paris, Venice, Biarritz and Cannes to the collection of bedrooms at her Villa *Madama* in Rome. Coop played it all calmly and quietly, and replenished his wardrobe in London and in Rome. When he returned to Hollywood, old friends found him looking something of a dude but otherwise the same quiet amiable fellow he'd been before embracing the international elite.

There was every reason for his serenity— Adolph Zukor, Paramount's production chief, had raised his salary to $1,750 a week and he was ready for the big time—*Morocco* with Josef von Sternberg directing Marlene Dietrich in her first English language film. Americans had been hearing of the daring blonde siren from Berlin but couldn't see her in *The Blue Angel*—the studio theory being that her ruthless character of Lola in the German movie would have a deleterious effect.

In 1930, audiences leaned to more sympathetic heroines, and certainly they were not yet ready for the Berlin they got around to discovering forty years later in *Cabaret*—hardly prepared for Lola's opening line when she peeks out the curtain of the dressing rooms and tells the others, "Stick your

Coop's last great role in "High Noon" with Grace Kelly won him his second Acadamy Award.

tits out, girls. Beautiful men are coming in." So *The Blue Angel*'s release was delayed until after *Morocco.*

In *Morocco*, Dietrich was given reverse casting—the role of a cabaret singer, accustomed to giving her favors to men in exchange for expensive baubles—until she meets Cooper as a French Foreign Legionaire. She taunts him with all the allure and sexual skills at her command. She begs him to desert the Legion, to choose her instead, but he refuses. Finally, desperate in her desire for the soldier, Dietrich turns her back on Adolphe Menjou, the rich lover willing to marry her and give her respectability. In the final scenes of the picture we see Marlene, chiffon whirling in the breeze, becoming a common camp follower, pursuing Cooper into the desert.

Morocco was the damndest movie—unadulterated trash—absurd—yet a triumph of casting and movie craftsmanship. No need for anyone who saw it the first time around to have his memory refreshed by television. The great scenes have been implanted as firmly as those in the Chaplin classics; Cooper, fingering Dietrich's jewels, Cooper's entrance, Arab women lifting their veils to show their faces, Dietrich's shoe slipping into the sand as, unmindful, she trudges in the wake of the marching Legionaires.

Never again did Gary Cooper approach the sensuousness he achieved in *Morocco*, and it appears to have been his own choice. He wasn't at all fooled by Von Sternberg, and he was aware that his character was being used as a male object of desire. Rene Jordan, a Cooper biographer, points out: "Cooper liked working with Dietrich, but risked suspension by turning down a co-starring role in *Dishonored*. He refused to work with von Sternberg. The Svengali-like director had exposed a side of Cooper's personality that he would rather have kept hidden. He had been led astray by *Morocco* but he would never again make a movie like this one."

* * *

Dorothy diFrasso enjoyed another year with Coop; this time luring him to Africa as part of a group she had organized to go on a safari. Dorothy was great at organizing things and people—putting them together in improbable situations. That had been her life style for so long, she assumed everyone else felt as she did. But Coop got fed up and came back to Hollywood ahead of schedule. One very important reason was his projected appearance opposite another fabled siren whom Paramount had imported from Europe by way of Alabama, the fabulous Tallulah Bankhead, who had been the sensation of London's "gallery girls" for the past several years—barely seen in her own country, but a legend nonetheless.

It was 1932, and Paramount couldn't have been more excited at snaring Tallulah. They put their best craftsmen to work on a screen adaptation of a Harry Harvey story (the adapter of Somerset Maugham's *Rain*), gave the script to Benn Levy, the direction to Marion Gering and signed two British newcomers for supporting roles, Cary Grant and Charles Laughton.

Grant's casting in the picture was barely accidental. Coop's frequent disappearances with the *Contessa*, timed to coincide with contract negotiations, had so unnerved the studio that they began looking around for a replacement. (In the era of the big studios, movie scripts were prepared with particular stars in mind. They couldn't be switched to suit just anybody's style of playing.) So when stars got huffy they began looking for substitutes. It wasn't an accident either that the movie name chosen for Archibald Leach came out as Cary Grant—a similarity Coop could hardly avoid noticing. But he'd learned to bluff his way through studio dealings. DiFrasso urged him on and he got a big raise before doing the Bankhead movie as well as the promise of Hemingway's *Farewell to Arms*.

The only movie of the era even approximating *The Devil and the Deep* as high camp was *The Cheat*, Tallulah's second picture, in which she bared her breast, showed Irving Pichel, the prosecuting attorney, a brand inflicted by her husband, screaming "This is what he did to me."

Audiences, unfortunately, didn't appreciate camp as they do today or *The Devil and the Deep* would have become an enormous success. Still, you couldn't go anywhere in New York without bumping into someone doing an impersonation of either Bankhead or Charles Laughton, the chief protagonists of the tangled love story. He was the commander of a submarine; Tallulah, his unfaithful wife and Gary and Cary, the fellows with whom the lady dallied. The submarine came to a bad end, but Tallulah floated up to the surface in a black chiffon nightgown.

Before Coop got his new contract of $7,500 a week underway Paramount forced him into cameo roles in *If I Had a Million* and *Alice in Wonderland*. The first remains a revival hit; the latter, a forgotten disaster.

Farewell to Arms failed to satisfy Hemingway, Cooper or readers of the novel. Assigned to Frank Borzage, a gentle director, best in fragile romantic dramas like *Seventh Heaven*, the hugeness of the Hemingway panorama was too much for Borzage. He turned the piece into a tender love story that audiences lapped up. They loved Coop and thought Helen Hayes was just wonderful. A tough, masculine story became a four-handkerchief women's picture and Paramount was ecstatic.

Cooper was thirty-two, the age at which all our *Giants*, Duke, Fonda and Stewart, reached career or personal turning points in their lives. In 1933 he met and proposed to a young actress called Sandra Shaw who was also a Social Register debutante, Veronica Balfe. The thirties became an awkward decade for debutantes—even those whose families had not been wiped out in the stock market crash. With the depression at its depth, they felt they *had* to do something. Many drifted to the arts, playing bit parts in New York or turning up in Hollywood as Sandra Shaw nee Veronica Balfe, "socialite-actress."

More devastating were the "society singers" who blossomed like ragweed in the empty depression-hit night clubs and hotel bars of New York's East Side. In Hattie Carnegie formals, they dangled ebony cigarette holders, and in husky, untrained voices sang things like *Smoke Gets In Your Eyes* as managers clustered around the door, praying their socially prominent names would at least entice some of their friends.

Once Coop and Veronica made up their minds that theirs was the real thing, Coop ended his relationship with the *Contessa*. There was a breezy finale to whatever had sprung up between him and Tallulah Bankhead. The lady from Alabama, for all her sophistication, had tumbleweed in her eye when she worked with Coop. In any event, Tallulah's movie days were destined to be short-lived; she returned to New York and the theatre.

There was one other intimate friendship to be terminated involving a dark-haired beauty not too often noted in Cooper biographies—lovely Evelyn Brent who seemed to show up in Coop's life between the more widely publicized loves—perhaps when he needed her. Underestimated as an actress, Evelyn drifted into the minor studios, then to smaller parts and finally disappeared into a quiet and happy marriage.

The marriage of Coop and Veronica was simple—only a few friends were present. No invitation was extended to the *Contessa*. She spent a lonely afternoon at the Cafe Vendome bar on Sunset Boulevard where she and Coop had dined in the patio so gaily in the yesterdays. She did not hide her disappointment or her tears as she sipped the "in" drink of the time—*creme de menthe frappe.*

By all the rules, losing Coop should have been the living end for Dorothy as far as Hollywood was concerned. Far from it. She came back year after year, and when the World War II drove cafe society out of Europe she chose a mansion in Beverly Hills while other Paris expatriates languished in New York and Palm Beach. As vivacious as ever, she became famous as a hostess with the mostest—and, with Pickfair on the wane, an invitation to Dorothy's was highly prized.

Having tasted the fruit of the Southland, Dorothy combed the trees for more. Her next "brief encounter" occurred at Santa Anita where she was introduced to a Mr. Benjamin Siegel, whose name had started appearing in the columns as a sportsman and business man friend of George Raft who had recently moved his family from New York to Beverly Hills.

Before you could say "Mah Jong," Mr. Siegel, compact, muscular, blue-eyed, a mop of curly black hair combed carefully to conceal a touch of baldness, sinister but damned attractive, could be found at Dorothy's side on the receiving line of her fabled parties. Once she turned her living room into a stadium, with a real boxing ring. Two pugs battled a few rounds to polite applause and the tinkle of champagne glasses.

Mr. Siegel smiled as he glanced at the crowd and wondered about his next conquests—beauties like

Marie MacDonald, Wendy Barrie and some others who chose not to be identified when Dottie woke up one morning to read that *her* Mr. Siegel had been arrested for conspiracy to commit murder and was being held in the County Jail by authorities who knew him better as Bugsy Siegel, one of the inventors of Murder, Inc.

Dorothy chartered a private plane to fly to San Simeon carrying a sapphire necklace which she intended offering William Randolph Hearst as security against a cash loan she wanted to bail Siegel out. Hearst, horrified, pitying the woman, turned her over to his secretary who quietly escorted Dorothy back to her plane.

Cooper never flinched when diFrasso's name was brought up in his presence. She simply had ceased to exist for him. He had nothing to say. Marriage to Rocky, as Veronica was nicknamed, had a salutary effect. He settled down completely, aware that his playboy days were over. It was time to build the Cooper "image".

Veronica's family had long since overcome objections to her marrying an actor with Coop's reputation for high living, a sort of wolf on the hoof. Neither suspicion was entirely true in respect to Coop. He was no Errol Flynn when it came to numbers. As for being *The Last of the Big Spenders*, that was impossible. Coop hadn't made that kind of money.

But it was in the cards. The Cooper image was beginning to grow. He had made his presence felt where it counted—at the boxoffice. Coop began his climb to the Big Ten, and when he reached the top

Coop, with his wife and daughter, in Copenhagen. Their private life was not always serene.

he stayed there. He had become one of the best known U.S. citizens in the world, raw-boned, noncommittal, casting a shadow a little taller than life with depths of humor and melancholy not immediately discernible to the desert-dazzled eye. He was a fellow who was slow to anger but quick on the draw, likely to gulp at his first sight of the great city but not taken in by it, bashful with women, but perfectly capable of deviltry if exposed to French perfume on Saturday nights.

* * *

One by one the Cooper pictures rolled out of Hollywood into the theatres of the world and with each release his stature increased. Even the dogs had quality written in them—put there by Cooper and the directors and writers who worked with him. *Mr. Deeds Goes to Town* started a run that went on to *The Plainsman* for C.B. DeMille, *Souls at Sea* with Henry Hathaway and unfortunately, a very poor choice to renew his old association with Samuel Goldwyn, the totally forgettable *The Adventures of Marco Polo*. Once more *Beau Geste* was filmed, with tough guy director William Wellman making it count as Cooper headed a cast that included Robert Preston, Ray Milland, Susan Hayward, Brian Donlevy and J. Carrol Naish.

In 1938, the Coopers had their first and only child, daughter Maria. The Coopers had moved into a Georgian house with three acres of land surrounding it, with a swimming pool, tennis courts and the things and animals that were important to the Coopers, dogs, ducks, chickens, citrus groves and a vegetable garden. In summer they either travelled abroad or lived on their estate on Long Island, an Eastern home, for a change of pace and climate and to keep the family in closer touch with Veronica.

Being rich came easily to Coop. He found he didn't have to make a big thing of it, as he'd been tempted to at the beginning of his career. He liked his old clothes, enjoyed fussing with his gun collection, indulging his other hobbies. One premiere was enough for Coop. They tore his clothes off when he attended the opening of *Design for Living* and, afterward, he avoided the more conspicuous Hollywood social occasions, limiting appearances to the Academy Awards and other functions that served the interests of the industry.

He and Veronica both avoided the night clubs which had been a part of his earlier Hollywood days. He'd had enough. Coop seldom drank but was a chain smoker of denicotinized cigarettes.

The only thing Coop never took for granted was his career. "You can't take chances in this business," he reminded himself and his agent whenever a new project came up. "You want to be as sure as you can that the thing is right." Things weren't always right—Coop couldn't expect perfection. But he liked to imagine that if the potential existed he would still come out ahead of the game.

Paramount and Cooper called it quits after he turned down Rudyard Kipling's *The Light That Failed* which Ronald Colman took—to his dismay. Coop was right. But for a long time, Coop had as bad luck with scripts as anyone else in Hollywood, as the screen struggled to keep up with a changing world covered by the clouds of war. No one really knew what kind of entertainment the public was going to buy. They were too preoccupied with new responsibilities that had suddenly been thrust upon them—through becoming, as President Roosevelt put it, "the arsenal of Democracy." Overnight, America, still fighting its way out of the depression, was becoming a vast factory for the production of planes and the munitions that went with them.

Meet John Doe and *Sergeant York* were Coop's highlights of this era of his career. *York* was a personal triumph for the actor—a characterization of a hero of World War I that won him, besides an Oscar, the vote of the New York critics as Best Actor of 1941. The film was credited with contributing a new understanding to the country's overwhelming isolationist attitude toward the war in Europe. It obliged people to take a second look at the facts and to realize we were living in a Fool's Paradise—as Pearl Harbor eventually dramatized with such shocking impact.

The war years were not good ones for Cooper, despite *The Story of Dr. Wassell* which Cecil DeMille directed. A story of the heroism of an Arizona doctor who led a group of wounded Marines to safety during the war in the Pacific, it failed to come off—due to DeMille's usual grandiose approach to what was basically a simple, uncomplicated story of an individual's bravery.

Pride of the Yankees disproved the old notion that baseball pictures were boxoffice poison—thanks to its central character, the late Lou Gehrig and the honesty of Cooper's performance. This was Cooper at his very best—and producer Samuel Goldwyn proving that his famed touch had not lost its magic.

But if Coop's career seemed to be extending itself longer than many leading men of the time, the star's marriage had disintegrated. For the sake of appearance and for their daughter, the Coopers maintained the illusion of a marriage which no longer existed. There was respect between the pair, but after twelve years the light had flickered out of the romance. It amounted to "one of those things."

Like many men of his age in the same predicament, Coop wasn't comfortable "fooling around." Although the probability that he did was not out of the question.

As things turned out, the safe assumption is that Coop began looking for someone else—a woman to take Rocky's place. That wouldn't be easy. Admittedly, the difference of their interests had strained the marriage. And when Rocky took a hand in his career, such as suggesting that Coop try working through his own production company, lining up with International, a quiet, friendly independent composed of top but not especially effective movie men, her advice boomeranged. International eventually merged with Universal, losing its identity.

When love struck Coop it came like a bolt from the blue—in the exciting newcomer Patricia Neal who arrived in Hollywood in 1947, fresh from a triumph on Broadway in Lillian Hellman's *Another Part of the Forest* which took another view of the Southern family Miss Hellman had dramatized so excitingly in *The Little Foxes* which established Tallulah Bankhead as a major American theatrical figure.

Miss Neal had come to New York from Packard, Kentucky, where she was born. Pat began life in a mining camp—her father was an official of the South Coal Company—but life among the miners wasn't nearly as rough as the penthouses and Beverly Hills mansions she was to encounter later. Her father sent her to Northwestern University, but she quit after two years and headed for Broadway, determined to become a star.

She was that one in a million who saw her name in lights along the Great White Way within the year she started. She landed in *Forest* and walked off with the Tony award as well as the New York drama critics' best actress award. There hadn't been a more talked-about performance in years—and justifiably so. The role was a *tour de force* for Patricia Neal.

Her signing with Warners on a long term contract coincided with a similar deal Coop had just made with the studio—a pact for six pictures which followed his disappointments at not making it on his own in the independent field.

A slim, sexy redhead with come-hither eyes and a husky, sensuous voice, she received the publicity buildup befitting a talented young actress with star billing on Broadway, rave notices in her scrap book and all the available awards. Pat Neal seemed a sure bet for stardom.

Any hopes that Pat Neal was going to make it the easy way were dashed with the announcement that the young actress had been chosen to play in Ayn Rand's *The Fountainhead*. Pat was only twenty or twenty-one, but she could read, and she should have been aware that the Rand novel had become a best-seller through a combination of *chutzpah*, horror, indignation, curiosity and disbelief. No one on this planet, outside of Ayn Rand, ever admitted finishing it.

Jack Warner must have been brain-washed that season, for he invited Miss Rand to do the screenplay, which emerged in a style best described as "tortured amateur night." King Vidor was signed to direct and being of the old school he didn't really believe in screenplays—preferring to doodle along in his own imaginative, often effective, sometimes disastrous fashion.

Vidor, at least, represented quality, and so did the cast. Humphrey Bogart, the original choice for the role of the highly individualistic architect hero of Miss Rand's wordy skyscraper novel would have nothing to do with the lady, so Cooper got the job. The property had been intended for Barbara Stanwyck, but Vidor considered her too old; hence the choice of Patricia Neal.

Bogie and Barbara were lucky. Cooper, who really never knew how to give a poor performance, got a lesson in this one as he labored through Miss Rand's jumbled philosophical dialogue, combed, it seems, from the combined works of Father

Coughlin, Gerald L.K. Smith and Kathleen Windsor. There is a love-hate relationship between Neal and Cooper that swings back and forth like a grandfather's clock, the scenes of passion all played against an Art Deco background of skyscrapers. Obviously, Vidor was having the time of his life as he compressed this mammoth piece of junk into a reasonable running time and got it off Jack Warner's hands and got Miss Rand out of town.

There have been worse pictures than *The Fountainhead*—but seldom from the same studio with the same combination of stars. Cooper and Neal co-starred again in an unbelievably awful melodrama called *Bright Leaf* which Warners carried to the farthest extremity of the Los Angeles area for its press preview. They feared it would be hooted off the screen at its proud, traditional Hollywood Boulevard showcase house.

Bright Leaf had some of *The Fountainhead* but more camp. It was about the tobacco industry, the tycoons who own it, their high-strung, half-mad daughters and the men who marry them to get a piece of the family fortune. Pat Neal, such a fine actress today, must cringe at the mere mention of *Bright Leaf* as she screamed her way through an imitation of Bette Davis and Miriam Hopkins that made Tallulah Bankhead's last appearances seem like underplaying. Lauren Bacall, as a proud sensitive prostitute who snares Cooper at the end, was the sole redeeming feature of the unbelievable exhibition.

There may have been behind-the-scenes reasons

for this dismal showing by an old pro and an untried screen actress, but that's fan magazine stuff. That Cooper had fallen head over heels in love with Pat had nothing to do with the front office choice of their vehicles.

If, as one biographer has pointed out, the romance plunged Coop and Pat into years of misery and despair, it comes as late news to the press corps who saw them frequently together— dining in cozy, out-of-the way spots, obviously enjoying themselves. No one bothered them. The press had too much respect for Coop, and laid off. One could hardly say the two lovers were hounded—unless it was by themselves.

Coop did lose some friends. A straying husband always does, as sympathy went to Rocky, staunch in her Catholicism and unwilling to agree to a divorce. The lovers found a hideaway in the hills where they lived together, looking for approval and finding it here and there. They visited Ernest Hemingway in Havana. Pat and Coop became Mr. and Mistress.

When a separation of the Coopers was announced, the press did move in, and it was commonly believed that Coop would find his own way out of the mess through a Mexican divorce in order to marry the younger woman. Warners got nervous about the Cooper image and rushed him into a series of quickies to conclude their contract.

They feared that the public could reject a tarnished Cooper. They still saw him as a young, tall-in-the-saddle young cowboy who neither smoked, drank or swore and always took off his ten-gallon hat in the presence of "ladies." Not as a fortyish man going through far from unusual problems.

Morality was a one-way street in Hollywood. Studio heads lived by one code—stars endured the ignominity of a morals clause in their contracts—subject to loose interpretation. Louis B. Mayer could chase starlets around his desk; Zanuck was free to collect new stars in Paris night club dens and Harry Cohn did whatever his thing happened to be—snarling at Rita Hayworth or scaring Kim Novak. They were all scared until Ingrid Bergman washed the nonsense down the sewer and emerged as Hollywood's first liberated heroine.

A man like Coop had to contend with the likes of Hedda and Louella—women who couldn't ruin him but could make life miserable with their sly innuendo. Theirs were the voices Jack Warner listened to when he told Cooper to "knock it off"—the voices of old, frustrated, tiresome women who got their power because producers like Warner handed it to them on a silver platter.

Today, such attitudes seem unbelievable, yet one wonders if Jack Warner's paternalistic knuckle-slapping wasn't more sensible in the long run than the Kafka world of today—when blithe comediennes like Carol Channing discover they head the enemies list of the President of the United States and a girl like Jane Fonda has a foot-thick dossier in the files of the F.B.I.

It all came to an end in 1951 and Coop went back to his home. Said Pat years later, "I got myself into a sticky mess which couldn't work, didn't work and never would have worked. He was the most gorgeously attractive man—bright too although some people didn't think so. I lived this secret life for several years.

"I was so ashamed, yet there was the fact of it. I made few close friends. And all I had in Hollywood was that one love."

And when it was over, Hollywood turned its back on the willowy redhead from Kentucky. She still made movies, but the parts were not designed to enhance her career. A statuesque 5 feet 8, she was cast opposite leading men inches shorter. She had to speak lines not intended for her deep, throaty voice. In a hundred ways, her studio bosses indicated they would be glad to get rid of her.

"I didn't drop Hollywood," she said. "It dropped me. Hollywood has a way of indicating to contract artists that it is fed up with them. Studios began to feed me all the bad parts."

Finally, Pat took the hint and returned to New York. Her promising career and her one big romance were shattered. She had to start all over again. But her good friend Lillian Hellman gave her a second chance at both acting and love.

While Pat was starring in a revival of the Hellman play, *The Children's Hour*, Lillian invited her to a party and introduced her to British writer Roald Dahl—the man she eventually married, who was at her side during the rest of the Greek tragedy Pat was obliged to play—the brain damage to her son from an automobile accident, the death of her seven-year-old daughter and the brain tumor that almost claimed Pat's life.

For Cooper there came *High Noon*, the rich role

of Will Kane, the about-to-be-retired Marshal who, on his wedding day, learns that desperadoes he has sent to jail have been released and are rushing back to kill him.

Instead of support from the town he has served for so many years, admiration from his new wife for his courage, the Marshal stands alone in the ultimate test of his manhood. He meets the criminals on the turf they've chosen; it is his Quaker wife who aims a rifle and fights at his side at the end. The townspeople rejoice and when they come to cheer and hail their hero he throws his Marshal's badge in the dust.

This was quality Cooper—the kind of three-dimensional hero his fans expected. And it didn't matter that Coop seemed suddenly to have aged before their eyes. He didn't care about his enemy the camera. He let the cragginess show; fire lit up his eyes only now and then. Coop's was a performance that came from within, giving it the aura of greatness. Cooper's second Oscar came the hard way.

* * *

In all the theatrical stories I've read or written I know of only one concerning an artist who found just the right moment to quit, picked it and kept her promise. She was Mary Garden, the first American singer to reach the heights in opera, in concert and into everyone's heart. She was a beauty as well as a great artist. Composers wrote for her and when she was asked her thoughts as she went on the stage in Paris for her debut there, she smiled and answered, "I said to myself, 'Tomorrow, Mary, all Paris will be at your feet.'" She was right.

Some years later at the peak of her fame, she was sitting in the wings at the Metropolitan Opera House during a performance of *The Juggler of Notre Dame*, an opera she adored singing, watching the dancer juggling in front of the statue of the Virgin. She wondered, "Why am I here? I've done it all—everything. There's nothing left—no more mountains to climb." Mary finished the performance, walked home, lost in her thoughts and that was the end of her career. She never sang again. She quit at her peak.

Coop was fifty-one when he won his Oscar for *High Noon* and the Cooper image had about run its course. It was time to pack it up and take time off—to come back now and then, if he wanted to, in character roles or cameo bits. He'd already done enough of the latter to know that sometimes they were fun.

But Coop couldn't. He went straight on, forcing photographers to filter his lined face with gauze. In 1958 he entered a Boston hospital for surgery and even the strongest denials never stilled the rumors that Coop had a facelift. Even so, there was a haggard look about him in *Ten Frederick Street* that shocked audiences. Something was radically wrong with Coop, but like a man possessed, he raced from picture to picture until he reached his final one in 1959, *The Naked Edge*.

The producer of *The Naked Edge* was Walter Seltzer, a man who had been around Hollywood in numerous capacities virtually all his adult life, closely associated with Hal Wallis, Warners,

Metro, and as producer for Charlton Heston and a number of other companies. In an *Esquire* interview, Seltzer gave readers a rare glimpse of Cooper—how he ticked, what made him work, his awareness of the Cooper mystique, the complete objectivity with which he viewed the qualities most responsible for his success. Said Seltzer:

"We had this idea for Cooper to make a switch. For him to play in a suspense picture and make him, Gary Cooper the suspect. So I called Cooper. He was in the West Indies and he got a copy of the book, read it, and signed the contract without ever seeing the screenplay. But, of course, he knew we had Joe Stefano who wrote the *Psycho* screenplay for Hitchcock. The financial arrangements were simple. Coop is the easiest deal in the world. He never figures in it. His agent or his lawyer handles the fiscal policy. Baroda Productions just gets so much money and a percentage of the profits. Then Coop had one meeting with Stefano and us before we started shooting. That's all he needs. We had this meeting with Coop in Paris about the story, the team, the plans. He was on his way to go skin-diving in the south of France with Rocky and Maria. He has a definite concept of himself as a hero. Definite. He wasn't sure the audience would accept him as a possible murderer. So we convinced him they would. He wanted certain lines changed in the script and certain things added to make his character softer. Like, in the first version, Stefano wanted to build up the fact that there was a warm, personal relationship at the outset between the hero and his wife, so he wrote in some cute little sexy lines. Coop said he couldn't deliver those lines. He said we'd get laughed out of the theatre. He said he can't deliver coy, sexy lines. So now, instead of those lines, we have different devices. For instance, we have a moment in an early scene where he's in court and she massages his shoulder. That shows the relationship Coop's way. There was another kind of scene which Stefano had in there where Coop was supposed to squeeze a tube of toothpaste into the lens of the camera. Coop said he couldn't do that either. Too phallic. And then, finally, Coop wanted bits here and there in the script that softened him, his character. So for example, after his testimony sends another man to jail, he mumbles to the man's wife: 'I'm sorry.' Just that, but it does a great deal. Well, it was that sort of thing. Coop knows what he wants. After the meeting, he gave us the name of his London tailor, said he'd see us two days before the shooting, and took off."

Coop's cancer had been discovered by the Boston doctors. But they didn't let him know. They performed two major abdominal operations within five weeks. He seemed quickly restored and in excellent spirits when he arrived in England for the Seltzer production. He was curious about the venture, doubtful that audiences would accept him as an assassin but willing to try. He was determined to stretch the Cooper image to its fullest.

He enjoyed London, the theatre and with his fondness for cars took special delight in the Rolls Royce the studio provided him with, especially the notion of riding around in a vehicle with bullet-proof glass. That appealed to his sense of humor.

In February, 1961, doctors finally told him the

221

truth about his cancer and began treating him with radioactive cobalt. Cooper managed to keep the news from spreading for three months, making it appear that his life was running at full steam as he visited Miami for the Patterson-Ingemar Johanssen heavyweight fight and attended Mass in Los Angeles on Easter Sunday with his family. He had been converted to Catholicism in 1953.

But at the Academy Awards ceremonies shortly thereafter it was obvious that something had gone wrong. Scheduled to receive his third Oscar, an honorary Award, not Coop, but Jimmy Stewart appeared on the stage to accept the coveted statuette. Stewart's voice broke as he said, "We're all terribly proud of you, Coop, terribly proud." Two days later his agent released the news of his mortal illness.

Cooper had the world's attention. He bore his illness with stoic fortitude and often blew his stack as he read the premature obituaries concealed as "Life stories." He remained remarkably composed and calm. Until the very last hours, when he was placed under heavy sedation, Coop was able to sit up, have a drink, talk to his family and friends. On May 14, 1961, seven days after his sixtieth birthday, Gary Cooper died.

Newspapers wrote admiringly of Cooper's long career as an American actor in the finest tradition, a man of his time, a legend. Wrote the London Times: "Cooper summed up the shifting American dream in terms of our national reluctance to grow older and our pioneer belief in the inevitable triumph of good over evil. On the screen he was essentially the simple man who resolved complexities by taking matters into his own hand and simplifying them. The critics of American cinema could look for clues in Cooper's films that often have mirrored our democratic mood if not our nature. He was the hero of *A Farewell to Arms* when we were preoccupied with pacifism, with the liberal-minded Mr. Deeds in the New Deal era, and both Sergeant York (pacifist turned warrior) and Robert Jordan (civilian turned guerrilla) in a world at war. He was a lonely hero in *High Noon* at the beginning of the Eisenhower era."

Life wrote: "Everywhere in the world people spoke of loss and tried to define precisely what was lost. 'Perhaps,' mourned *Corriere della Serra*, Italy's most important newspaper, 'with him there is ended a certain America...that of the frontier and of innocence which had or was believed to have an exact sense of the dividing line between good and evil.'

"Wrote the *Svenska Dagbladet*: 'He had the soul of a boy, a pure, simple, nice, warm boy...he was the incarnation of the honorable American.'

"'In a way,' commentated Hamburg's *Die Welt*, 'he had been a key figure of our days...He was the symbol of trust, confidence and protection...He is dead now. What a miracle that he existed.'"

Life's own tribute said: "In his thirty-six years as a public figure Gary Cooper was the sort of American other Americans would somehow like to have been and never more so than this spring."